POEMS BY:
Lexie Botzum
Jessica Spencer

Arielle Stein
Claire Abramovitz

MW00736504

poem
hashavuah

Published by Ben Yehuda Press
122 Ayers Court #1B
Teaneck, NJ 07666
http://www.BenYehudaPress.com

To subscribe to our monthly book club and support independent Jewish publishing, visit https://www.patreon.com/BenYehudaPress

Jewish Poetry Project #39   **http://jpoetry.us**

Ben Yehuda Press books may be purchased at a discount by synagogues, book clubs, and other institutions buying in bulk.
For information, please email markets@BenYehudaPress.com

ISBN13 978-1-953829-57-3 paper

23 24 25 / 10 9 8 7 6 5 4 3 2   20231015

Foreword

I was inspired to begin this project by my friend Jess Spencer, who spent a year writing a poem for every parsha. I decided it would be a good way to ensure both *b'iyun* (in-depth) weekly parsha study and *kavua* (fixed/regular) creative writing.

Every week I learned the parsha on Sefaria, flipping through 20-30 tabs of *mefarshim* and *midrash* on each line—trying to achieve the most holistic and rich view of the parsha possible, trying to find material that stuck with me, inspired me.

Much of the *midrash* and *parshanut* I found myself most caught on were those expanding or weaving anew stories of women the original text mentioned only in passing, or relegated to a footnote; and those examining the intricacies of romantic and familial relationship, both between humans and between the complicated triangle of Moshe, Hashem, and B'nei Yisrael.

I found myself moved and enchanted by these stories hiding beneath each *pasuk*, and still left with a lingering sense of dissatisfaction. Oftentimes, these stories of marginalized characters were learned out by the very fact of their absence. These stories and interpretations lend the text greater depth, but cannot simply make up for the silence in which they were born.

Nonetheless, I hadn't anticipated how these poems would make me feel. In spinning together disparate threads of *midrash*, putting *pesukim* and *gemarot* in conversation, placing myself in the head of Chava, Sarah, Miriam, Moshe, Hashem (heretical as it may be)—I found myself in the chain of transmission and creation. Giving voice to unarticulated interpretations and stories, weaving yourself into the text, is a way of claiming ownership. Rather than crouching beneath the text, we expand it. *L'hagdil torah v'yadir.*

I'd also like to note that these poems drew inspiration not only from midrash, parshanut, etc., but also from an array of divrei torah I've read over the past few years. The brilliant individuals writing these—some friends, some teachers, some strangers—had already provided their own incredible syntheses of the texts, which helped inform my readings and writings. Having these divrei torah to accompany my parsha learning over the years has lent incredible depth, and allowed me to be in conversation with voices both ancient and contemporary.

By collaborating with Arielle Stein, who produced gorgeous and deeply representative artwork (and later Claire Abramovitz, who produced several more stunning pieces), and Jess Spencer, who contributed her poems, I hoped to make something that can draw other people into this process. I hope that this parsha booklet can supplement people's learning and exploration; that the sources and thoughts shared here can serve as a starting point for further study. I want to share some of the means I've found for engaging deeply and earnestly with the text, and enable others to better engage with material that may feel inaccessible or alienating.

Happy reading.

-Lexie

Some Notes

I have changed masculine God language to gender-neutral God language wherever I found it in the sources, though occasionally poems gender God as either male or female. G-d is spelled sometimes with a dash, and sometimes without. This is a result both of copy-and-pasting from sources with different *shitot* and of my own inconsistency! I am large & I contain multitudes.

Also, for convenience's sake I have listed all *parshiyot* that often are read as double *parshiyot* in their joint form, though some poems were written on only one of the two parshas.

Finally, the poems written by Jessica Spencer are indicated with a symbol in the top corner of the page, and the artwork by Claire Abramovitz with All other poems are by Lexie Botzum, and all other drawings by Arielle Stein.

Table of Contents

Genesis

Exodus

Leviticus

Table of Contents (cont.)

Numbers

Deuteronomy

BEREISHIT

they stopped listening after *b'etzev teildi banim*

staring at each other and clutching hands, his eyes

bright and her body soft and swollen beneath each

draping fig leaf. God said *I will make great your pain*

in childbirth and they heard only, *you will birth children*

thought only, of the gentle thumping in her soft, swollen

stomach, as Hashem declared the land cursed Adam kissed

her feverishly, and when They'd decreed *vehu yimshol*

bakh Adam was stroking her cheekbones with fingers that

quivered, joyful and exploratory. they never heard it, see,

that they'd one day return to dust. and so Adam called her

mother of all life, the great maker & unmaker. and so when

Chava bore a son, with every contraction breathed life into a

figure of dust and ashes, she declared *kaniti ish et adonai*—

I have acquired Man, I have become like God.

Genesis 3:16

אֶל־הָאִשָּׁה אָמַר הַרְבָּה אַרְבֶּה עִצְּבוֹנֵךְ וְהֵרֹנֵךְ בְּעֶצֶב תֵּלְדִי בָנִים וְאֶל־אִישֵׁךְ תְּשׁוּקָתֵךְ וְהוּא יִמְשָׁל־בָּךְ:

And to the woman They said, "I will make most severe Your pangs in childbearing.
In pain shall you bear children. Yet your urge shall be for your husband, And he shall
rule over you."

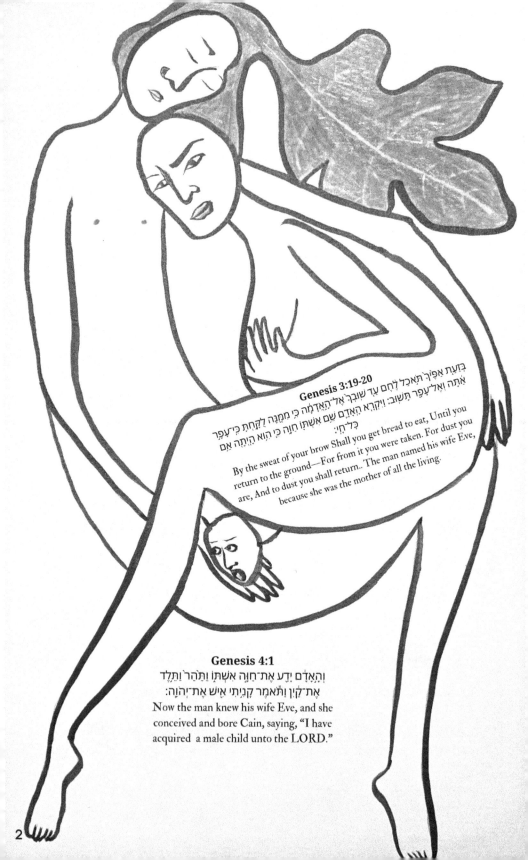

Genesis 3:19-20

בְּזֵעַת אַפֶּ֙יךָ֙ תֹּ֣אכַל לֶ֔חֶם עַ֤ד שֽׁוּבְךָ֙ אֶל־הָ֣אֲדָמָ֔ה כִּ֥י מִמֶּ֖נָּה לֻקָּ֑חְתָּ כִּֽי־עָפָ֣ר אַ֔תָּה וְאֶל־עָפָ֖ר תָּשֽׁוּב: וַיִּקְרָ֧א הָֽאָדָ֛ם שֵׁ֥ם אִשְׁתּ֖וֹ חַוָּ֑ה כִּ֛י הִ֥וא הָֽיְתָ֖ה אֵ֥ם כָּל־חָֽי:

By the sweat of your brow Shall you get bread to eat, Until you return to the ground—For from it you were taken. For dust you are, And to dust you shall return.. The man named his wife Eve, because she was the mother of all the living.

Genesis 4:1

וְהָ֣אָדָ֔ם יָדַ֖ע אֶת־חַוָּ֣ה אִשְׁתּ֑וֹ וַתַּ֙הַר֙ וַתֵּ֣לֶד אֶת־קַ֔יִן וַתֹּ֕אמֶר קָנִ֥יתִי אִ֖ישׁ אֶת־יְהֹוָֽה:

Now the man knew his wife Eve, and she conceived and bore Cain, saying, "I have acquired a male child unto the LORD."

2

IT IS NOT GOOD
TO BE ALONE
SO YOU SPLIT US
WATER FROM WATER
LIGHT FROM DARK.
WE CALLED YOU GOD.

WE PLUCKED FRUIT
AND GOOD AND EVIL BROKE
IN TWO. AT THE GATE
YOU CREATED OUTSIDE.
NOW I KNOW WHAT IT IS
TO BE ALONE.

Genesis 1:4

וַיַּרְא אֱלֹהִים אֶת־הָאוֹר כִּי־טוֹב וַיַּבְדֵּל אֱלֹהִים בֵּין הָאוֹר וּבֵין הַחֹשֶׁךְ׃

And God saw that the light was good and They distinguished between the light and the darkness.

Genesis 2:18

וַיֹּאמֶר יְהוָה אֱלֹהִים לֹא־טוֹב הֱיוֹת הָאָדָם לְבַדּוֹ אֶעֱשֶׂה־לּוֹ עֵזֶר כְּנֶגְדּוֹ׃

And the Lord God said, "It is not good for Man to be alone. I will make him a fitting helper."

Noach

By man is man's blood shed
said the Rememberer
Keeper of Words.
and Noah said nothing
but raised the rain-soaked gangway and hid
inside, smothered by smells
of dung and tar.

tell me, Lord
Creator
Destroyer of Worlds
how could I rest
when below me only waves
move over bloated bodies
of the wicked?

Blessed be the faithful.
Bless the Keeper of Worlds.

Mishneh Torah, Blessings 10:16

הָרוֹאֶה קֶשֶׁת בֶּעָנָן מְבָרֵךְ בָּרוּךְ אַתָּה יְיָ' אֱלֹהֵינוּ מֶלֶךְ הָעוֹלָם זוֹכֵר הַבְּרִית וְנֶאֱמָן בִּבְרִיתוֹ וְקַיָּם בְּמַאֲמָרוֹ.

One who sees a rainbow in the clouds blesses: "Blessed are You, God, king of the universe, who remembers the covenant, is faithful to Their covenant, and maintains Their word.

Bereshit Rabbah 3:7

אָמַר רַבִּי יְהוּדָה בַּר סִימוֹן, יְהִי עֶרֶב אֵין כְּתִיב כָּאן, אֶלָּא וַיְהִי עֶרֶב, מִכָּאן שֶׁהָיָה סֵדֶר זְמַנִּים קֹדֶם לְכֵן. אָמַר רַבִּי אַבָּהוּ מְלַמֵּד שֶׁהָיָה בּוֹרֵא עוֹלָמוֹת וּמַחֲרִיבָן, עַד שֶׁבָּרָא אֶת אֵלּוּ, אָמַר דֵּין הַנְיָן לִי, יַתְהוֹן לָא הַנְיָן לִי.

Rabbi Judah bar Simon said: it does not say, 'It was evening,' but 'And it was evening.' Hence we derive that there was a time-system prior to this. Rabbi Abbahu said: This teaches us that God created worlds and destroyed them, saying, 'This one pleases me; those did not please me.'

it's okay, you know—
I, too, have often begun
my projects without heeding
others' warnings, have charged
recklessly and hopefully into a path
of possibility and creation, have known
there lay equal potential for growth and
destruction, and so tipped the scales—
slightly.

one always hopes to be proven right,
in these cases; don't you wish
you could have held us before the
melakhim on your palm, cupped us
gently and uncurled your fingers before
emet and *shalom*, watched the wonder as
it crept across their faces, slowly.

it must have hurt to admit that
you had failed—that in all your
perfection, you had made something
too deeply imperfect, that you had
tipped the scales and watched the earth
lurch wildly out of control.

is this why you qualified your
promise, when you swore to
Noah—hedge your bets and fill
the sky with fractured light, tell
the *melakhim* we are a failed project
that you have nonetheless chosen
to continue.

Genesis 8:21

וַיָּ֣רַח יְהוָה֮ אֶת־רֵ֣יחַ הַנִּיחֹחַ֒ וַיֹּ֨אמֶר יְהוָ֜ה אֶל־לִבּ֗וֹ לֹֽא־אֹ֠סִף לְקַלֵּ֨ל
ע֤וֹד אֶת־הָֽאֲדָמָה֙ בַּעֲב֣וּר הָֽאָדָ֔ם כִּ֠י יֵ֣צֶר לֵ֧ב הָאָדָ֛ם רַ֖ע מִנְּעֻרָ֑יו
וְלֹֽא־אֹסִ֥ף ע֛וֹד לְהַכּ֥וֹת אֶת־כָּל־חַ֖י כַּאֲשֶׁ֥ר עָשִֽׂיתִי׃

The LORD smelled the pleasing odor, and the LORD said to
Himself: "Never again will I doom the earth because of man,
since the devisings of man's mind are evil from his youth; nor
will I ever again destroy every living being, as I have done."

5

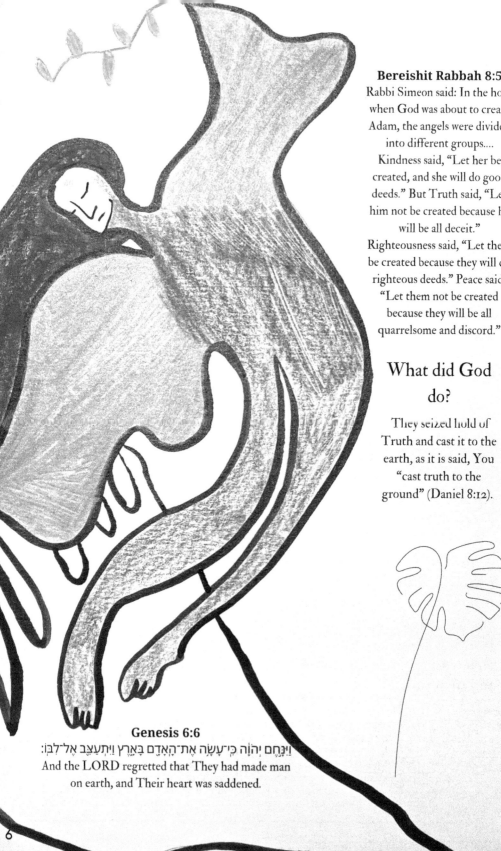

Bereishit Rabbah 8:5
Rabbi Simeon said: In the hour when God was about to create Adam, the angels were divided into different groups.... Kindness said, "Let her be created, and she will do good deeds." But Truth said, "Let him not be created because he will be all deceit." Righteousness said, "Let them be created because they will do righteous deeds." Peace said, "Let them not be created because they will be all quarrelsome and discord."

What did God do?

They seized hold of Truth and cast it to the earth, as it is said, You "cast truth to the ground" (Daniel 8:12).

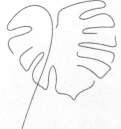

Genesis 6:6
וַיִּנָּחֶם יְהוָה כִּי־עָשָׂה אֶת־הָאָדָם בָּאָרֶץ וַיִּתְעַצֵּב אֶל־לִבּוֹ׃
And the LORD regretted that They had made man on earth, and Their heart was saddened.

Lekh Lekha

you chose him as Abram brought
him out from Ur Chasdim and shaped
his name new in your mouth Abraham
for *h*ashem Abraham a new man
and we can never call him by his old
name call him by his first name but
we do, every day—

you change your name line to line
we call you *elohim* adonai tzvaot
el shaddai el elyon *shekhinah* yhwh
ha-shem, the name, *kel*'s and tetra-
grammatons tripping off our tongues
and they all trace the barest outline
of you, edges left gaping by the names
we still don't know—

but we each only get one.
one name to be born with,
one name to wrap around us
as shield and shelter, one name from
us or one name from you and once the
hey the *ha-shem* is inserted there's
no going back—this is me, now.

only you're given the *reshut* to contain
multitudes, to be simultaneously everything
you are, have been, will be, might be;
Hagar knew her name was fixed, knew
the ה lived already on the tip of her tongue her
outline already filled in with mis-placed-ness
and her son's name stolen from her mouth,
but *you*—you she could plant a new
name in like a flag, call out *el-roi*—

god who sees me.
and boldly, simply, she named herself
anew in your eyes.

Genesis 17:5

וְלֹא־יִקָּרֵא עֹוד אֶת־שִׁמְךָ אַבְרָם וְהָיָה שִׁמְךָ
אַבְרָהָם כִּי אַב־הֲמֹון גֹּויִם נְתַתִּיךָ:

And you shall no longer be called Abram,
but your name shall be Abraham, for I
make you the father of a multitude of
nations.

Berakhot 13a

Also, with regard to Abraham's name, bar
Kappara taught: Anyone who calls Abraham
Abram transgresses a positive mitzva, as it is
stated: "And your name will be Abraham"
(Genesis 17:5). This is a positive mitzva to
refer to him as Abraham. Rabbi Eliezer says:
One who calls Abraham Abram transgresses
a negative mitzva, as it is stated: "And your
name shall no longer be called Abram, and
your name will be Abraham, for I have made
you the father of a multitude of nations"
(Genesis 17:5).

Nechemia 9:7, read in Pesukei D'Zimra (Morning Prayer)

אַתָּה־הוּא יְי וָוֹה הָאֱלֹהִים אֲשֶׁר
בָּחַרְתָּ בְּאַבְרָם וְהֹוצֵאתֹו מֵאוּר
כַּשְׂדִּים וְשַׂמְתָּ שְּׁמֹו אַבְרָהָם:

You are the LORD God, who
chose Abram, who brought
him out of Ur of the
Chaldeans and changed his
name to Abraham.

7

Genesis 16:11

וַיֹּאמֶר לָהּ מַלְאַךְ יְהֹוָה הִנָּךְ הָרָה וְיֹלַדְתְּ בֵּן וְקָרָאת שְׁמוֹ יִשְׁמָעֵאל כִּי־שָׁמַע יְהֹוָה אֶל־עׇנְיֵךְ:

The angel of the Lord said to her further, Behold, you are with child and shall call bear a son; you shall call him Ishmael, for the Lord has paid heed to your suffering.

Genesis 16:13

וַתִּקְרָא שֵׁם־יְהֹוָה הַדֹּבֵר אֵלֶיהָ אַתָּה אֵל רֳאִי כִּי אָמְרָה הֲגַם הֲלֹם רָאִיתִי אַחֲרֵי רֹאִי:

And she called the LORD who spoke to her, "You Are El-roi," by which she meant, "Have I not gone on seeing after They saw me!"

Genesis 12:11-13
וַיְהִ֕י כַּאֲשֶׁ֥ר הִקְרִ֖יב לָב֣וֹא מִצְרָ֑יְמָה וַיֹּ֙אמֶר֙ אֶל־שָׂרַ֣י אִשְׁתּ֔וֹ הִנֵּה־נָ֣א יָדַ֔עְתִּי כִּ֛י אִשָּׁ֥ה יְפַת־מַרְאֶ֖ה אָֽתְּ: וְהָיָ֗ה כִּֽי־יִרְא֤וּ אֹתָךְ֙
הַמִּצְרִ֔ים וְאָמְר֖וּ אִשְׁתּ֣וֹ זֹ֑את וְהָרְג֥וּ אֹתִ֖י וְאֹתָ֥ךְ יְחַיּֽוּ: אִמְרִי־נָ֖א אֲחֹ֣תִי אָ֑תְּ לְמַ֙עַן֙ יִֽיטַב־לִ֣י בַעֲבוּרֵ֔ךְ וְחָיְתָ֥ה נַפְשִׁ֖י בִּגְלָלֵֽךְ:

As he was about to enter Egypt, he said to his wife Sarai, "I know/have realized what a beautiful woman you are. If
the Egyptians see you, and think, 'She is his wife,' they will kill me and let you live. Please say that you are my sister,
that it may go well with me because of you, and that I may remain alive thanks to you."

catch me swimming in a chest of
golden coins, see that I am so
glorious and fearful and afraid—
you'll see that nestled amongst
them in the river's reflection I look,
almost, like the sun look, almost, like
a Goddess; maybe you'll contemplate
finding more gold simply to complement
my hair and I, I will never forgive you

I am born aloft as treasure.

catch me wreathed in golden silk,
facing the mirror glorious and fearful
and burning—there is an angel by my
shoulder and to him I call "Smite!" and
to him I call "Smite!" and I stand in
a house crumbling about me, bend down
to swiftly, softy, lace my sandals; you'll
see me ride out of the ruins in the midst
of your glorious great and golden new herds
and you'll think, perhaps you should bow.

Midrash Tanchuma, Lekh Lekha 5:1-2
When they reached the Egyptian border, and were standing on the bank of the Nile, our patriarch
Abraham noticed that Sarah's reflection in the river was like the radiance of the sun... He told her: "The
Egyptians are a dissolute lot, for it is written of them: Whole flesh is as the flesh of asses (Ezek. 23:20),
and so, I will hide you in this cabinet and lock it, for I fear for my safety if the Egyptians should see
you." He did so. As he was about to cross the Nile, the tax-collectors gathered about him and asked:
"What are you carrying in the cabinet?" "Barley," he replied. They retorted: "It is not barley, but
wheat." "Then charge me the duty for wheat," said he. "But it may be pepper," they argued. "Then take
the tax for pepper," he insisted. They said to him: "It must be gold coins." Finally, they compelled him
to open the box. When they beheld her countenance, which was as radiant as the sun, they said to him:
"Truly, she is not meant for a commoner."

Midrash Tanchuma, Lekh Lekha 5:3

And the Lord plagued Pharaoh and his house with great plagues because of the word of Sarai (Gen. 12:17). What is indicated by the phrase Because of the word of Sarai? An angel descended with a staff from heaven at that moment, and when Pharaoh later approached her to remove her shoe, he struck him upon the hand, and when he approached to touch her clothing, the angel struck him again.

However, the angel consulted Sarah before administering each blow.

How do we know that? We know that because it is written: Because of the word of Sarai. Scripture does not say "Because of" or "For the sake of" or "On account of her merit," but simply, "Because of the word of Sarai." If Sarah told the angel to strike him, he struck him, and if she told him to desist, momentarily, he desisted.

Genesis 12:16

וּלְאַבְרָם הֵיטִיב
בַּעֲבוּרָהּ וַיְהִי־לוֹ
צֹאן־וּבָקָר וַחֲמֹרִים
וַעֲבָדִים וּשְׁפָחֹת
וַאֲתֹנֹת וּגְמַלִּים׃

And because of her, it went well with Abram; he acquired sheep, oxen, asses, male and female slaves, she-asses, and camels.

Vayera

I didn't laugh—or maybe I did, but it was only
for a moment you couldn't have heard it or barely
barely because it was just that, a moment, a breathy
chuckle and an *oh* of surprise because can you imagine,
something broken creating wholeness, oh the impossibility,
but I didn't laugh, really truly, when he said *no* you laughed I
said perhaps he imagined it, perhaps he had already stolen the
laughter of my son's name, perhaps he willed this very moment
into being. I told you I believed him but you weren't meant to believe
me—to believe that I could really, really truly set myself up for such
breathtaking disappointment; you should have known I wouldn't release
this breath till I felt my belly swell, found presence in the place of void;

I laughed when that boy was born because I felt joy, because I felt that release,
finally, of a breath held 12 months, and because I knew, that when you stood upon
that mountaintop inventing prayer, when you found that prayer existed in the
space of hurt and disappointment and devastation, you didn't even think to pray for me.

Genesis 18:12-15

וַתִּצְחַק שָׂרָה בְּקִרְבָּהּ לֵאמֹר אַחֲרֵי בְלֹתִי הָיְתָה־לִּי עֶדְנָה וַאדֹנִי זָקֵן: וַיֹּאמֶר יְהוָה אֶל־אַבְרָהָם לָמָּה זֶּה צָחֲקָה שָׂרָה לֵאמֹר הַאַף אֻמְנָם אֵלֵד וַאֲנִי זָקַנְתִּי: הֲיִפָּלֵא מֵיהוָה דָּבָר לַמּוֹעֵד אָשׁוּב אֵלֶיךָ כָּעֵת חַיָּה וּלְשָׂרָה בֵן: וַתְּכַחֵשׁ שָׂרָה | לֵאמֹר לֹא צָחַקְתִּי כִּי | יָרֵאָה וַיֹּאמֶר | לֹא כִּי צָחָקְתְּ:

And Sarah laughed to herself, saying, "Now that I am withered, am I to have enjoyment—with my husband so old?" Then the LORD said to Abraham, "Why did Sarah laugh, saying, 'Shall I in truth bear a child, old as I am?' Is anything too wondrous for the LORD? I will return to you at the same season next year, and Sarah shall have a son." Sarah lied, saying, "I did not laugh," for she was frightened. But They replied, "You did laugh."

Genesis 17:19

וַיֹּאמֶר אֱלֹהִים אֲבָל שָׂרָה אִשְׁתְּךָ יֹלֶדֶת לְךָ בֵּן וְקָרָאתָ אֶת־שְׁמוֹ יִצְחָק וַהֲקִמֹתִי אֶת־בְּרִיתִי אִתּוֹ לִבְרִית עוֹלָם לְזַרְעוֹ אַחֲרָיו:

God said, "Nevertheless, Sarah your wife shall bear you a son, and you shall name him Isaac; and I will maintain My covenant with him as an everlasting covenant for his offspring to come."

It was taught in a baraita in accordance with the opinion of Rabbi Yosei, son of
Rabbi Hanina: Abraham instituted the morning prayer, as it is stated when
Abraham came to look out over Sodom the day after he had prayed on its behalf:
"And Abraham rose early in the morning to the place where he had stood before
the Lord" (Genesis 19:27), and from the context as well as the language utilized in
the verse, the verb standing means nothing other than prayer.

When should I have stopped looking?

When the flames leapt from the ropes
to my daughter's hair
should I have closed my eyes?

When he pushed my daughters into the street
should I have turned away?

When the city burnt—
oh, my daughters, how it burnt—
should I have not looked back?

Salt pillar by a dead sea
I stand witness and wait
for the return of my daughter's daughter
and the true judge to bring justice at last.

Genesis 18:25

חָלִלָה לְּךָ מֵעֲשֹׁת | כַּדָּבָר הַזֶּה לְהָמִית צַדִּיק עִם־רָשָׁע וְהָיָה כַצַּדִּיק
כָּרָשָׁע חָלִלָה לָּךְ הֲשֹׁפֵט כָּל־הָאָרֶץ לֹא יַעֲשֶׂה מִשְׁפָּט:

Far be it from You to do such a thing, to bring death upon
the innocent as well as the guilty, so that innocent and guilty
fare alike. Far be it from You! Shall not the Judge of all the
earth deal justly?

Pirkei d'Rabbi Eliezer 25:8

Rabbi Yehudah said: They announced in Sodom: Everyone who strengthens the
hand of the poor or the needy with a loaf of bread shall be burnt by fire. Paltit,
daughter of Lot, was married to one of the great men of Sodom. She saw a
certain poor man in the street of the city, and her soul grieved for him, as it is
said, "Was not my soul grieved for the needy?" (Job 30:25). What did she do?
Every day when she went out to draw water she put in her bucket all sorts of
provisions from her home, and she fed that poor man. The men of Sodom said:
How does this poor man live? When they discovered the matter, they brought her
forth to be burnt with fire.

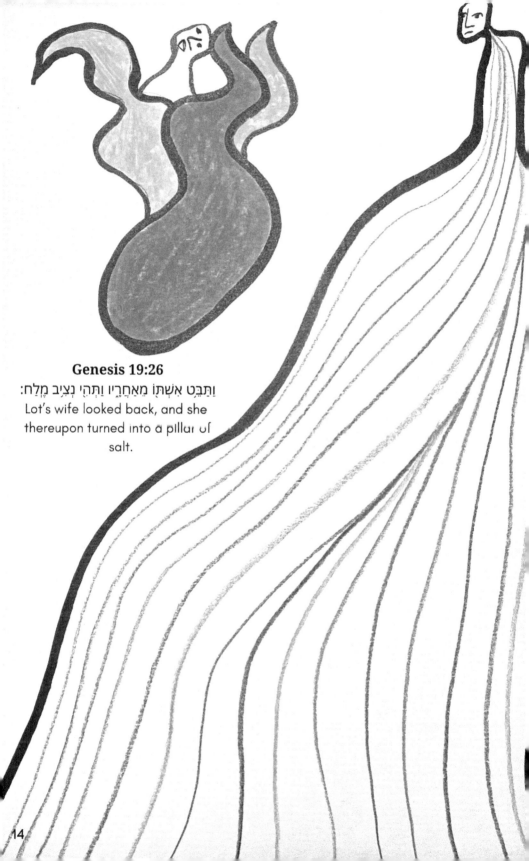

Genesis 19:26

וַתַּבֵּט אִשְׁתּוֹ מֵאַחֲרָיו וַתְּהִי נְצִיב מֶלַח:

Lot's wife looked back, and she thereupon turned into a pillar of salt.

Chayei Sarah

I fell off a camel when I first
saw you, your eyes rising to meet
us, my eyes rising to meet yours,
and you were so lost and so open
and so sweet—it felt like meeting a
friend, and it felt like being chosen,
and it felt like being the first, maybe,
to discover love, and so when you
picked up your pace and hurried toward
us I thought *I am home* and I thought
I am ready to dismount, that is to say,
I am ready to fall.

Genesis 24:64
וַתִּשָּׂא רִבְקָה אֶת־עֵינֶיהָ וַתֵּרֶא
אֶת־יִצְחָק וַתִּפֹּל מֵעַל הַגָּמָל׃
Raising her eyes, Rebekah saw
Isaac. She alighted (lit. fell) from
the camel.

Genesis 24:67
וַיְבִאֶהָ יִצְחָק הָאֹהֱלָה שָׂרָה אִמּוֹ וַיִּקַּח אֶת־רִבְקָה וַתְּהִי־לוֹ לְאִשָּׁה
וַיֶּאֱהָבֶהָ וַיִּנָּחֵם יִצְחָק אַחֲרֵי אִמּוֹ׃
Isaac then brought her into the tent of his mother Sarah, and he
took Rebekah as his wife. Isaac loved her, and thus found comfort
after his mother's death

Author's Note:
Yitzchak is the first person in Tanakh to be described as loving someone. On Alicia
Jo Rabins' "Girls in Trouble" album, the song "I Fell Off My Camel" is a poignant
instrumental piece, an "imagined soundtrack for the moment when Rebecca first
sees her future husband Isaac." She points out that while most mepharshim explain
"falling" here to mean dismounting, falling off one's camel is an incredible image for
love at first sight.

Toldot

As a boy, my father's knife
blinded me with tears
from heaven. I never
saw clearly after that.

God called
(God of my father)
told me where to live
(as sworn to my father)
blessed me
(in the name of my father)
and I sinned and grew rich
as had my father.

I could not see what son
would want this legacy
but both claimed it, in the end.
A father's birthright
and a life lived on the edge
of a blade.

Genesis 25:31
וַיֹּאמֶר יַעֲקֹב מִכְרָה כַיּוֹם
אֶת־בְּכֹרָתְךָ לִי:
Jacob said [to Esau],
"First sell me your
birthright."

Bereshit Rabbah 65:10
שֶׁבְּשָׁעָה שֶׁעָקַד אַבְרָהָם אָבִינוּ
אֶת בְּנוֹ עַל גַּבֵּי הַמִּזְבֵּחַ בָּכוּ
מַלְאֲכֵי הַשָּׁרֵת, הֲדָא הוּא דִכְתִיב
(ישעיה לג, ז): הֵן אֶרְאֶלָּם צָעֲקוּ
חֻצָה וגו', וְנָשְׁרוּ דְמָעוֹת
מֵעֵינֵיהֶם לְתוֹךְ עֵינָיו, וְהָיוּ
רְשׁוּמוֹת בְּתוֹךְ עֵינָיו, וְכֵיוָן
שֶׁהִזְקִין כָּהוּ עֵינָיו, הֲדָא הוּא
דִכְתִיב: וַיְהִי כִּי זָקֵן יִצְחָק, וגו'
At the time that our father
Abraham bound his son on
the altar, the serving angels
wept, as it is written: "the
angels of peace weep
bitterly." And tears fell from
their eyes into Isaac's eyes,
and left traces in his eyes. As
he aged, his eyes faded, as
it is written: "When Isaac was
old and his eyes were too
dim to see."

Vayetzei

I see angels ascending and
descending upon your
stomach, Leah,
their hands pressing so
softly,
and Leah,
your eyes were perfect
in the womb till an
angel kissed them
closed and sealed in
all your Torah,
and Leah,
Rachel was jealous of
your righteousness, your
soft walk & kind sons &
you have to know,
Leah,
that you deserve to be
someone's first choice,
that you shouldn't need to
bargain for their love, or
win it with your offerings,
with each umbilical cord
cut.

and Leah Immeinu,
you have to know,
G-d didn't open your
womb because she didn't
want your prayers—
she just couldn't bear
to see you suffer.

Genesis 29:17
וְעֵינֵי לֵאָה רַכּוֹת וְרָחֵל הָיְתָה יְפַת־תֹּאַר וִיפַת מַרְאֶה:
Leah had weak eyes; Rachel was shapely and beautiful.

Radak on Genesis 29:17
The eyes of Leah were soft: She was beautiful, but her eyes were soft and teary.

Genesis 28:12
וַיַּחֲלֹם וְהִנֵּה סֻלָּם מֻצָּב אַרְצָה וְרֹאשׁוֹ מַגִּיעַ הַשָּׁמָיְמָה וְהִנֵּה מַלְאֲכֵי אֱלֹהִים עֹלִים וְיֹרְדִים בּוֹ:
[Ya'akov] had a dream; a stairway was set on the ground and its top reached to the sky, and angels of God were going up and down on it.

Bereishit Rabbah 45:4
Why were the matriarchs barren? Rabbi Levi said in Rabbi Shila's name and Rabbi Chelbo in R. Yochanan's name: Because the Holy One of Blessing yearns for their prayers and conversations (sichatan), as it is written 'O my dove, you on the clefts of the rock let Me see your face, let Me hear your voice' (Song of Songs 2:14): Why did I make you barren? In order to 'see your face... hear your voice.'

Genesis 29:31
וַיַּרְא יְהוָה כִּי־שְׂנוּאָה לֵאָה וַיִּפְתַּח אֶת־רַחְמָהּ וְרָחֵל עֲקָרָה:
The LORD saw that Leah was unloved and They opened her womb; but Rachel was barren.

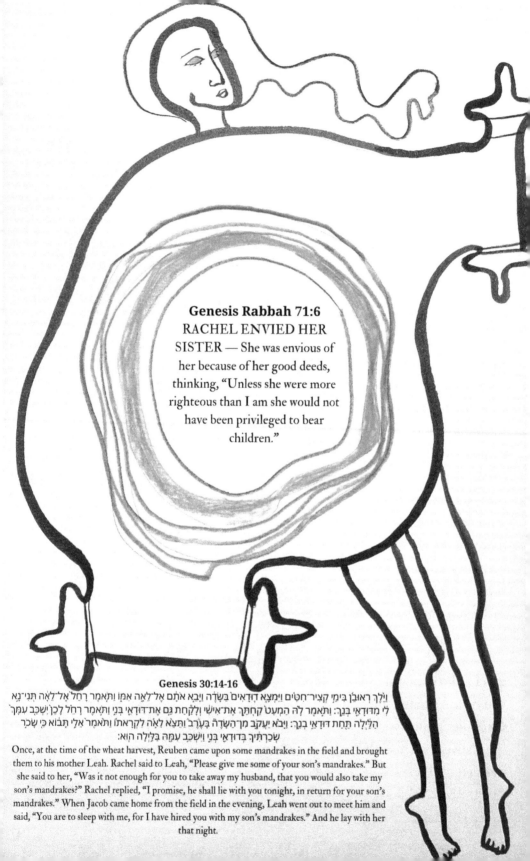

Genesis Rabbah 71:6
RACHEL ENVIED HER
SISTER — She was envious of
her because of her good deeds,
thinking, "Unless she were more
righteous than I am she would not
have been privileged to bear
children."

Genesis 30:14-16

וַיֵּ֨לֶךְ רְאוּבֵ֜ן בִּימֵ֣י קְצִיר־חִטִּ֗ים וַיִּמְצָ֤א דֽוּדָאִים֙ בַּשָּׂדֶ֔ה וַיָּבֵ֣א אֹתָ֔ם אֶל־לֵאָ֖ה אִמּ֑וֹ וַתֹּ֤אמֶר רָחֵל֙ אֶל־לֵאָ֔ה תְּנִי־נָ֣א
לִ֔י מִדּוּדָאֵ֖י בְּנֵֽךְ: וַתֹּ֣אמֶר לָ֗הּ הַמְעַט֙ קַחְתֵּ֣ךְ אֶת־אִישִׁ֔י וְלָקַ֕חַת גַּ֥ם אֶת־דּוּדָאֵ֖י בְּנִ֑י וַתֹּ֣אמֶר רָחֵ֗ל לָכֵן֙ יִשְׁכַּ֤ב עִמָּךְ֙
הַלַּ֔יְלָה תַּ֖חַת דּוּדָאֵ֥י בְנֵֽךְ: וַיָּבֹ֨א יַעֲקֹ֣ב מִן־הַשָּׂדֶה֮ בָּעֶרֶב֒ וַתֵּצֵ֨א לֵאָ֜ה לִקְרָאת֗וֹ וַתֹּ֙אמֶר֙ אֵלַ֣י תָּב֔וֹא כִּ֣י שָׂכֹ֤ר
שְׂכַרְתִּ֔יךָ בְּדוּדָאֵ֖י בְּנִ֑י וַיִּשְׁכַּ֥ב עִמָּ֖הּ בַּלַּ֥יְלָה הֽוּא:

Once, at the time of the wheat harvest, Reuben came upon some mandrakes in the field and brought
them to his mother Leah. Rachel said to Leah, "Please give me some of your son's mandrakes." But
she said to her, "Was it not enough for you to take away my husband, that you would also take my
son's mandrakes?" Rachel replied, "I promise, he shall lie with you tonight, in return for your son's
mandrakes." When Jacob came home from the field in the evening, Leah went out to meet him and
said, "You are to sleep with me, for I have hired you with my son's mandrakes." And he lay with her
that night.

Vayishlach

He saw her. He lay with her. He took
her. She who went to see the daughters
of the land, unsistered daughter of four mothers,
she who went out
he took her.

He was a chief's son,
he was drawn to her, he said
he loved her, he said
sweet words to her.
He raped her.

The girl born alone
the woman named judgement,
how did she judge her brothers
who took the women
of Shechem? I don't know.
Her words left the page,
were taken from her, and
she went out.

Genesis 34:1-3

וַתֵּצֵא דִינָה בַּת־לֵאָה אֲשֶׁר
יָלְדָה לְיַעֲקֹב לִרְאוֹת בִּבְנוֹת
הָאָרֶץ: וַיַּרְא אֹתָהּ שְׁכֶם
בֶּן־חֲמוֹר הַחִוִּי נְשִׂיא הָאָרֶץ
וַיִּקַּח אֹתָהּ וַיִּשְׁכַּב אֹתָהּ
וַיְעַנֶּהָ: וַתִּדְבַּק נַפְשׁוֹ בְּדִינָה
בַּת־יַעֲקֹב וַיֶּאֱהַב אֶת־הַנַּעֲרָ
וַיְדַבֵּר עַל־לֵב הַנַּעֲרָ:

Now Dinah, the daughter
whom Leah had borne to
Jacob, went out to visit
the daughters of the land.
Shechem son of Hamor
the Hivite, chief of the
country, saw her, and took
her and lay with her and
violated her. Being
strongly drawn to Dinah
daughter of Jacob, and in
love with the maiden, he
spoke to the maiden
tenderly.

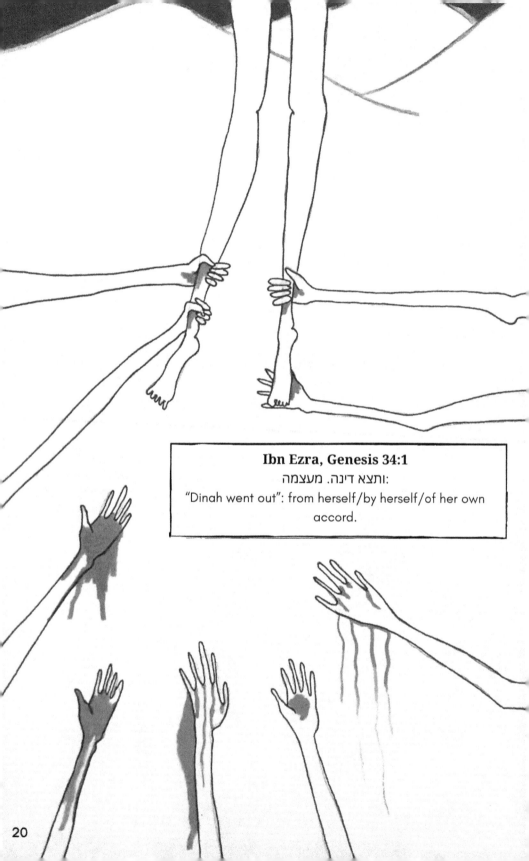

Ibn Ezra, Genesis 34:1
ותצא דינה. מעצמה:
"Dinah went out": from herself/by herself/of her own accord.

Ramban on Genesis 32:8
THEN JACOB WAS GREATLY AFRAID.
This was because they told him that Esau had gone forth from his city and...took along many men — four hundred. He thus greatly feared for his life, for he said, "He has not taken all these men except for the purpose of waging war against me."

Chizkuni on Genesis 32:7
AND WITH HIM ARE FOUR HUNDRED MEN.
He took them along to honor you.

Genesis 32:10-11
וַיֹּאמֶר֮ יַעֲקֹב֒ אֱלֹהֵי֙ אָבִ֣י אַבְרָהָ֔ם וֵאלֹהֵ֖י אָבִ֣י יִצְחָ֑ק יְהֹוָ֞ה הָאֹמֵ֣ר אֵלַ֗י שׁ֤וּב לְאַרְצְךָ֙ וּלְמוֹלַדְתְּךָ֔ וְאֵיטִ֖יבָה עִמָּֽךְ: קָטֹ֜נְתִּי מִכֹּ֤ל הַחֲסָדִים֙ וּמִכׇּל־הָ֣אֱמֶ֔ת אֲשֶׁ֥ר עָשִׂ֖יתָ אֶת־עַבְדֶּ֑ךָ...
Then Jacob said, "O God of my father Abraham's [house] and God of my father Isaac's [house], O Hashem, who said to me, 'Return to your native land and I will deal bountifully with you!' I am unworthy (*katonti*) of all the kindness that You have so steadfastly shown Your servant..."

Bereishit Rabbah 77:3
"A man began to wrestle with him." Rabbi Chama bar Chanina said, this was the ministering angel of Esau.

Genesis 32:27
וַיֹּ֣אמֶר שַׁלְּחֵ֔נִי כִּ֥י עָלָ֖ה הַשָּׁ֑חַר וַיֹּ֙אמֶר֙ לֹ֣א אֲשַֽׁלֵּחֲךָ֔ כִּ֖י אִם־בֵּרַכְתָּֽנִי:
Then [the figure] said, "Let me go, for dawn is breaking." But [Jacob] answered, "I will not let you go, unless you bless me."

Genesis 33:4
וַיָּ֨רׇץ עֵשָׂ֤ו לִקְרָאתוֹ֙ וַֽיְחַבְּקֵ֔הוּ וַיִּפֹּ֥ל עַל־צַוָּארָ֖ו וַׄיִּׄשָּׁׄקֵ֑ׄהׄוּׄ וַיִּבְכּֽוּ:
Esau ran to greet him. He embraced him and, falling on his neck, he kissed him; and they wept.

seeing your face is
like seeing the face
of G-d and
katonti
I am unworthy of
you *katonti* I am
made small by your
kindness and your offers
to help to guide *katonti*
I thought you had brought
men for my death not my
honor *katonti* I wrested a
brakha from your angel because
I needed to feel worthy
katonti
you have made me feel less
worthy and *katonti* my
fear has rendered me too
small to miss you

fall upon my neck
and weep, sink your
teeth into my veins—
I'll bleed out my
apologies.

Genesis 33:10
וַיֹּ֣אמֶר יַעֲקֹ֗ב אַל־נָא֙ אִם־נָ֨א מָצָ֤אתִי חֵן֙ בְּעֵינֶ֔יךָ וְלָקַחְתָּ֥ מִנְחָתִ֖י מִיָּדִ֑י כִּ֣י עַל־כֵּ֞ן רָאִ֣יתִי פָנֶ֗יךָ כִּרְאֹ֛ת פְּנֵ֥י אֱלֹהִ֖ים וַתִּרְצֵֽנִי:
But Jacob said, "No, I pray you; if you would do me this favor, accept from me this gift; for to see your face is like seeing the face of God, and you have received me favorably."

Bereishit Rabbah 78:9
[The word] 'kissed' is dotted [above each letter in the Torah's writing]...Rabbi Yannai said to him: ...On the contrary, it teaches that [Esav] came not to kiss [Yaakov] but to bite him, but our ancestor Yaakov's neck became like marble and that wicked man's teeth were blunted.

Vayeshev

Yosef, she's sitting in the
ohel Rachel sweeping her
hair up
gently,
telling her that she is
beautiful, telling her that
she is strong, telling her that
the world is not always kind
to girls who dream

and Yosef, his father's
favorite, toddling after
Ya'akov clutching his
legs wrapped snugly,
hiding,
in a wild spotted tunic dragging
behind him, slightly,
in the dust—

and Yosef, whispering to
her brothers that's she's dreamed
a dream and not heeding
her mother's advice because
maybe, if they know,
if she can *tell* them with
words that are still not
the right words,
they'll understand and

Yosef, huddled in a
pit's dark corner because
they couldn't understand,

Yosef now sitting cross-
legged before the mirror
in a strange man's home curling
her hair with soft nimble
fingers and brushing faint
rouge on each cheek thinking
maybe, it is better not
tucking herself away and
maybe, she should've unwrapped
her hair long ago and now
Ya'akov may never *know* and

Yosef, a second garment of
his torn from him dangling
from a strange woman's fingers
and this time he can *run*
and run and

Yosef, again hidden in the
dark and thinking maybe,
her mother was right about
young girls' dreams and
thinking maybe, her mouth
should remain shut her hair
remain covered her face
remain hidden but thinking
maybe, still,

it'll turn out better this time.

Author's Note:

This poem is inspired
by Nurit Zerachi's
poem היא יוסף ("She is
Joseph"), which
envisions Rachel
lying about Joseph's
gender to avoid the
shame of having still
not born a boy. Such
a read is likely
inspired by, among
other things, Joseph's
more "feminine"
characteristics—his
care for appearance
and clothing, his
emotional
vulnerability, etc. I
believe there is value
in the presence of
biblical men that
overturn certain toxic
masculine tropes, but
am also moved by
Zerachi's read.

Genesis 37:3
וְיִשְׂרָאֵל אָהַב אֶת־יוֹסֵף
מִכָּל־בָּנָיו כִּי־בֶן־זְקֻנִים הוּא לוֹ
וְעָשָׂה לוֹ כְּתֹנֶת פַּסִּים:
Now Israel loved Joseph best
of all his sons—he was his
"child of old age"; and he
had made him an
ornamented tunic.

Genesis 37:5
וַיַּחֲלֹם יוֹסֵף חֲלוֹם וַיַּגֵּד לְאֶחָיו וַיּוֹסִפוּ עוֹד שְׂנֹא אֹתוֹ:
Once Joseph had a dream which he told to his brothers; and they
hated him even more.

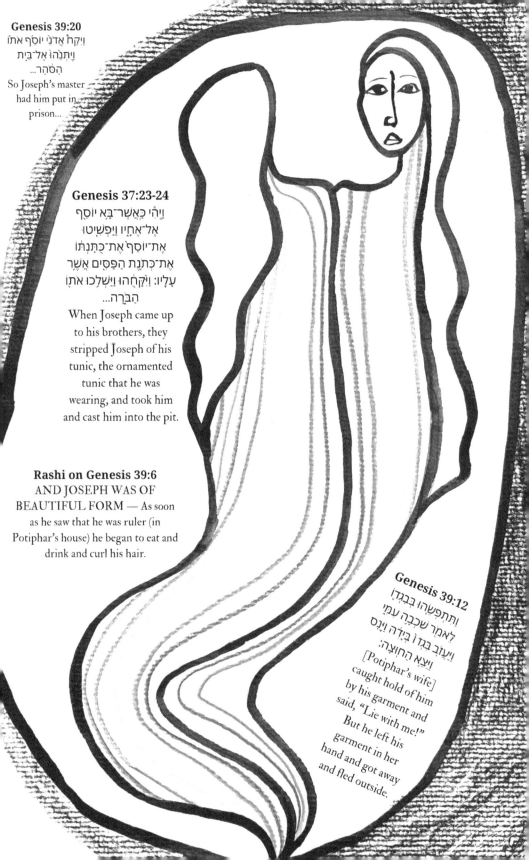

Genesis 39:20
וַיִּקַּ֞ח אֲדֹנֵ֤י יוֹסֵף֙ אֹת֔וֹ וַֽיִּתְּנֵ֙הוּ֙ אֶל־בֵּ֣ית הַסֹּ֔הַר...
So Joseph's master had him put in prison...

Genesis 37:23-24
וַֽיְהִ֕י כַּֽאֲשֶׁר־בָּ֥א יוֹסֵ֖ף אֶל־אֶחָ֑יו וַיַּפְשִׁ֤יטוּ אֶת־יוֹסֵף֙ אֶת־כֻּתָּנְתּ֔וֹ אֶת־כְּתֹ֥נֶת הַפַּסִּ֖ים אֲשֶׁ֥ר עָלָֽיו׃ וַיִּ֨קָּחֻ֔הוּ וַיַּשְׁלִ֥כוּ אֹת֖וֹ הַבֹּ֑רָה...
When Joseph came up to his brothers, they stripped Joseph of his tunic, the ornamented tunic that he was wearing, and took him and cast him into the pit.

Rashi on Genesis 39:6
AND JOSEPH WAS OF BEAUTIFUL FORM — As soon as he saw that he was ruler (in Potiphar's house) he began to eat and drink and curl his hair.

Genesis 39:12
וַתִּתְפְּשֵׂ֧הוּ בְּבִגְד֛וֹ לֵאמֹ֖ר שִׁכְבָ֣ה עִמִּ֑י וַיַּעֲזֹ֤ב בִּגְדוֹ֙ בְּיָדָ֔הּ וַיָּ֖נָס וַיֵּצֵ֥א הַחֽוּצָה׃
[Potiphar's wife] caught hold of him by his garment and said, "Lie with me!" But he left his garment in her hand and got away and fled outside.

Miketz

if you can imagine for a moment,
me crouching amidst the cactus and
the thorns, a charm around my neck
and a crown in my curls—can you
imagine me covered in dust, crouched
amidst bushes and hearing no voice of
God but my own. when I was borne to
Egypt on angel's wings, you can imagine
me lovely and lost, a lone woman with leather
skin. when I saw you ride past with your curls
and coat of many colors, your feet littered
with flowers and burnished arm bracelets, I
stood in front of the horse and he halted,
right there. you peered round his head to see
why you'd stopped so abruptly, only to find that
your horse had been wise—he knew, to stop before
a cluster of thorns. come prick yourself on my fingers—
I will draw you out, slowly.

Genesis 41:45
וַיִּקְרָ֨א פַרְעֹ֣ה שֵׁם־יוֹסֵף֮ צָֽפְנַ֣ת פַּעְנֵ֒חַ֒
וַיִּתֶּן־ל֣וֹ אֶת־אָֽסְנַ֗ת בַּת־פּ֥וֹטִי פֶ֛רַע כֹּהֵ֥ן אֹ֖ן
לְאִשָּׁ֑ה וַיֵּצֵ֥א יוֹסֵ֖ף עַל־אֶ֥רֶץ מִצְרָֽיִם:
Pharaoh then gave Joseph the name
Zaphenath-paneah; and he gave him
for a wife Asenath daughter of Poti-
phera, priest of On. Thus Joseph
emerged in charge of the land of Egypt.

Chizukuni Genesis 41:45

This quotes Pirkei de Rabbi Eliezer chapter 38 according to which [Osnat] was the daughter of Dinah who had been raped by Shechem, her very name suggesting that she was the product of rape. Having been raised in the house of a high official such as Potiphar, and bearing his name, would help to remove any stigma from her.

According to the Midrash, after her birth Yaakov expelled her, placing a golden plate around her neck inscribed with the Holy Name and hiding her among some cactuses and similar prickly plants,

so that when found she was named according to the location where she had been found— סנה, "thornbush."

The angel Gavriel brought her to Egypt and presented her to the wife of Potiphar, where she was raised. When Joseph was paraded after his ascension to power and all the young women of Egypt crowded around him to admire his being so handsome (49:22), and throwing flowers at him, Osnat, who had no flowers, threw her charm at him. When Joseph took a look at the inscription on that charm, he realised that she was the daughter of his half sister Dinah, and decided to marry her.

Vayigash

Midrash Tanchuma, Vayetzei 10:2
Similarly, as long as Jacob resided in Laban's home, the divine word did not reveal itself to him, even though They had assured him: And, behold, I am with thee (Gen. 28:15).

Genesis 32:27-29

וַיֹּאמֶר שַׁלְּחֵנִי כִּי עָלָה הַשָּׁחַר וַיֹּאמֶר לֹא אֲשַׁלֵּחֲךָ כִּי אִם־בֵּרַכְתָּנִי: וַיֹּאמֶר אֵלָיו מַה־שְּׁמֶךָ וַיֹּאמֶר יַעֲקֹב: וַיֹּאמֶר לֹא יַעֲקֹב יֵאָמֵר עוֹד שִׁמְךָ כִּי אִם־יִשְׂרָאֵל כִּי־שָׂרִיתָ עִם־אֱלֹהִים וְעִם־אֲנָשִׁים וַתּוּכָל:

Then [the angel] said, "Let me go, for dawn is breaking." But he answered, "I will not let you go, unless you bless me." Said the [angel], "What is your name?" He replied, "Jacob." Said he, "Your name shall no longer be Jacob, but Israel, for you have striven with beings divine and human, and have prevailed."

Genesis 32:32

וַיִּזְרַח־לוֹ הַשֶּׁמֶשׁ כַּאֲשֶׁר עָבַר אֶת־פְּנוּאֵל וְהוּא צֹלֵעַ עַל־יְרֵכוֹ:

The sun rose upon him (lit. "for him") as he passed Penuel, limping on his hip.

Genesis 37:32-34

וַיְשַׁלְּחוּ אֶת־כְּתֹנֶת הַפַּסִּים וַיָּבִיאוּ אֶל־אֲבִיהֶם וַיֹּאמְרוּ זֹאת מָצָאנוּ הַכֶּר־נָא הַכְּתֹנֶת בִּנְךָ הִוא אִם־לֹא: וַיַּכִּירָהּ וַיֹּאמֶר כְּתֹנֶת בְּנִי חַיָּה רָעָה אֲכָלָתְהוּ טָרֹף טֹרַף יוֹסֵף: וַיִּקְרַע יַעֲקֹב שִׂמְלֹתָיו וַיָּשֶׂם שַׂק בְּמָתְנָיו וַיִּתְאַבֵּל עַל־בְּנוֹ יָמִים רַבִּים:

They had the ornamented tunic taken to their father, and they said, "We found this. Please examine it; is it your son's tunic or not?" He recognized it, and said, "My son's tunic! A savage beast devoured him! Joseph was torn by a beast!" Jacob rent his clothes, put sackcloth on his loins, and observed mourning for his son many days.

Genesis 45:26-27

וַיַּגִּדוּ לוֹ לֵאמֹר עוֹד יוֹסֵף חַי וְכִי־הוּא מֹשֵׁל בְּכָל־אֶרֶץ מִצְרָיִם וַיָּפָג לִבּוֹ כִּי לֹא־הֶאֱמִין לָהֶם: וַיְדַבְּרוּ אֵלָיו אֵת כָּל־דִּבְרֵי יוֹסֵף אֲשֶׁר דִּבֶּר אֲלֵהֶם וַיַּרְא אֶת־הָעֲגָלוֹת אֲשֶׁר־שָׁלַח יוֹסֵף לָשֵׂאת אֹתוֹ וַתְּחִי רוּחַ יַעֲקֹב אֲבִיהֶם:

And they told him, "Joseph is still alive; yes, he is ruler over the whole land of Egypt." His heart went numb, for he did not believe them. But when they recounted all that Joseph had said to them, and when he saw the wagons that Joseph had sent to transport him, the spirit of their father Jacob revived.

---

he spent twenty years in the dark, hands grasping for empty women and freckled sheep and crawling babes, for twenty years he worked his hardest and didn't hear a word from God.

when he spoke his name and wrenched away a new blessing, the sun shone on him, twisted and whole and new. it said *we've missed you* and *we've missed you.*

a beautiful blood-soaked tunic stole the light again; its brilliance leeched the rest of the world black. for twenty years he wrestled with no one, folded smooth hands in a placant lap and felt empty, maybe blind, maybe done.

true his father could not see between him and his brother but he, oh he could not see his sons at all.

his quiet empty heart stopped when he heard the news–perhaps he'd just forgotten what the day light looked like. perhaps he'd lost the space for all this spirit. perhaps he'd forgotten his own name.

Ramban Genesis 45:26
'VAYAPHAG' HIS HEART. His heart passed away and ceased to believe; his heart took no notice of their words.

Radak Genesis 45:27
AND HIS SPIRIT REVIVED. His spirit which had been as dead from shock, now revived. Our sages have said that the "spirit" mentioned in our verse which was revived in Yaakov was the spirit of prophetic insights which had departed from him 22 years ago when Joseph had been sold. We have an ancient tradition, amply documented in history, that in the absence of joy in one's life a person cannot enjoy such a spirit of prophecy.

Rabbeinu Bahya on Genesis 45:28
YISRAEL SAID. As long as his prophetic spirit had not been restored to him, the Torah referred to him only as Yaakov. Now that he had regained this additional spiritual dimension he is once more referred to as Yisrael.

Radak on Genesis 46:2
AND [G-D] SAID "YAAKOV YAAKOV." The reason this call to Yaakov is repeated is to illustrate that for how many years Yaakov had not been favoured with a communication from G'd.

By repeating his name at this point, Yaakov was alerted to the fact that he would receive a prophetic insight.

27

Vayechi

queen who redeems me,
bless the young girls—
that they might give teaching
blessing and curse with their
arms outstretched and
uncrossed—

may the blessings they give
themselves when no one else
will grant them be as teeming
multitudes upon the earth;

may they sit still and alert
by the sleeping lion, prey
lying in the dust at their feet.

Genesis 48:13-14

וַיִּקַּח יוֹסֵף֙ אֶת־שְׁנֵיהֶ֔ם אֶת־אֶפְרַ֨יִם
בִּֽימִינוֹ֙ מִשְּׂמֹ֣אל יִשְׂרָאֵ֔ל וְאֶת־מְנַשֶּׁ֥ה
בִשְׂמֹאל֖וֹ מִימִ֣ין יִשְׂרָאֵ֑ל וַיַּגֵּ֖שׁ אֵלָֽיו:
וַיִּשְׁלַח֩ יִשְׂרָאֵ֨ל אֶת־יְמִינ֜וֹ וַיָּ֣שֶׁת עַל־רֹ֣אשׁ
אֶפְרַ֨יִם֙ וְה֣וּא הַצָּעִ֔יר וְאֶת־שְׂמֹאל֖וֹ
עַל־רֹ֣אשׁ מְנַשֶּׁ֑ה שִׂכֵּל֙ אֶת־יָדָ֔יו כִּ֥י
מְנַשֶּׁ֖ה הַבְּכֽוֹר:

Joseph took the two of them,
Ephraim with his right hand—to
Israel's left—and Manasseh with his
left hand—to Israel's right—and
brought them close to him. But
Israel stretched out his right hand
and laid it on Ephraim's head,
though he was the younger, and his
left hand on Manasseh's head—thus
crossing his hands—although
Manasseh was the first-born.

Genesis 48:15-16

וַיְבָ֣רֶךְ אֶת־יוֹסֵף֮ וַיֹּאמַר֒ הָֽאֱלֹהִ֗ים אֲשֶׁר֩ הִתְהַלְּכ֨וּ אֲבֹתַ֤י לְפָנָיו֙ אַבְרָהָ֣ם וְיִצְחָ֔ק הָֽאֱלֹהִים֙ הָרֹעֶ֣ה אֹתִ֔י
מֵעוֹדִ֖י עַד־הַיּ֥וֹם הַזֶּֽה: הַמַּלְאָךְ֩ הַגֹּאֵ֨ל אֹתִ֜י מִכָּל־רָ֗ע יְבָרֵךְ֮ אֶת־הַנְּעָרִים֒ וְיִקָּרֵ֤א בָהֶם֙ שְׁמִ֔י וְשֵׁ֥ם אֲבֹתַ֖י
אַבְרָהָ֣ם וְיִצְחָ֑ק וְיִדְגּ֥וּ לָרֹ֖ב בְּקֶ֥רֶב הָאָֽרֶץ:

And he blessed Joseph saying,
"The God in whose ways my fathers Abraham and Isaac walked,
the God who has been my shepherd from my birth until this day–
the Messenger who has redeemed me from all harm–
Bless the lads.
In them may my name be recalled,
And the names of my fathers Abraham and Isaac,
And may they be as teeming multitudes upon the earth."

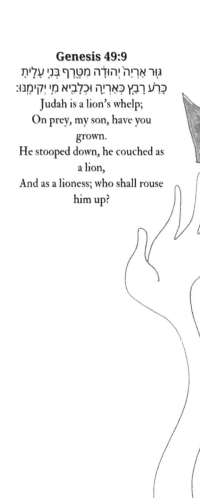

Genesis 49:9

גּוּר אַרְיֵה יְהוּדָה מִטֶּרֶף בְּנִי עָלִיתָ כָּרַע רָבַץ כְּאַרְיֵה וּכְלָבִיא מִי יְקִימֶנּוּ׃

Judah is a lion's whelp;
On prey, my son, have you grown.
He stooped down, he couched as a lion,
And as a lioness; who shall rouse him up?

Ezekiel 19:2

וְאָמַרְתָּ מָה אִמְּךָ לְבִיָּא בֵּין אֲרָיוֹת רָבָצָה בְּתוֹךְ כְּפִרִים רִבְּתָה גוּרֶיהָ׃

and say:
What a lioness was your mother among the lions!
Crouching among the great beasts,
she reared her cubs.

Author's Note:

I love HaMalakh HaGoel. It's a gorgeous prayer with a gorgeous tune. But I would like to bless the girls.

29

Shemot

I'm not sure that I would've turned to the fire with such stubborn astonishment. I think perhaps I'd have cast off my sandals and stood there frozen with uncertainty, toeing the line of sacred and profane.

Exodus 3:2-5

וַיֵּרָ֠א מַלְאַ֨ךְ יְהֹוָ֥ה אֵלָ֛יו בְּלַבַּת־אֵ֖שׁ מִתּ֣וֹךְ הַסְּנֶ֑ה וַיַּ֗רְא וְהִנֵּ֤ה הַסְּנֶה֙ בֹּעֵ֣ר בָּאֵ֔שׁ וְהַסְּנֶ֖ה אֵינֶ֥נּוּ אֻכָּֽל: וַיֹּ֣אמֶר מֹשֶׁ֔ה אָסֻֽרָה־נָּ֣א וְאֶרְאֶ֔ה אֶת־הַמַּרְאֶ֥ה הַגָּדֹ֖ל הַזֶּ֑ה מַדּ֖וּעַ לֹא־יִבְעַ֥ר הַסְּנֶֽה: וַיַּ֥רְא יְהֹוָ֖ה כִּ֣י סָ֣ר לִרְא֑וֹת וַיִּקְרָא֩ אֵלָ֨יו אֱלֹהִ֜ים מִתּ֣וֹךְ הַסְּנֶ֗ה וַיֹּ֛אמֶר מֹשֶׁ֥ה מֹשֶׁ֖ה וַיֹּ֥אמֶר הִנֵּֽנִי: וַיֹּ֖אמֶר אַל־תִּקְרַ֣ב הֲלֹ֑ם שַׁל־נְעָלֶ֙יךָ֙ מֵעַ֣ל רַגְלֶ֔יךָ כִּ֣י הַמָּק֗וֹם אֲשֶׁ֤ר אַתָּה֙ עוֹמֵ֣ד עָלָ֔יו אַדְמַת־קֹ֖דֶשׁ הֽוּא:

A messenger of יהוה appeared to him in a blazing fire out of a bush. He gazed, and there was a bush all aflame, yet the bush was not consumed. Moses said, "I must turn aside to look at this marvelous sight; why doesn't the bush burn up?" When יהוה saw that he had turned aside to look, God called to him out of the bush: "Moses! Moses!" He answered, "Here I am." And [God] said, "Do not come closer! Remove your sandals from your feet, for the place on which you stand is holy ground!"

Vaera

present yourself to
Pharaoh next morning as
he emerges from the water,
dripping,
hair loose—
you've never seen
it loose before—
and plastered to his
skin, tell him as
he hoists himself up
the bank that the
locusts will come crawling
from the earth beneath
his fingertips, yes
that earth, the very same,
that they'll fill your
field your court your house
your beds, mouths, noses—
tell him they'll
be inescapable.
clutch your rod and
stand firm and unsure
as he towels himself
off, meticulously,
ties it below his stubborn
heart and smoothes back his
hair, and tell him
that this is the cost of
his obstinance—

to be ruler over a land
of the dead and dying,
the spoiled and rotten.
tell him the stench will
creep even under his
doorways. tell him the
lice will crouch beneath
his pillow. tell him
your demand.

he will wrap himself
in golden robes, tuck
his hair beneath his
nemes, slip on his
sandals. the pharaoh
will appraise you,
and refuse.

Exodus 7:14-16

וַיֹּאמֶר יְהוָה אֶל־מֹשֶׁה כָּבֵד לֵב פַּרְעֹה מֵאֵן לְשַׁלַּח הָעָם: לֵךְ אֶל־פַּרְעֹה בַּבֹּקֶר הִנֵּה יֹצֵא הַמַּיְמָה וְנִצַּבְתָּ לִקְרָאתוֹ עַל־שְׂפַת הַיְאֹר וְהַמַּטֶּה אֲשֶׁר־נֶהְפַּךְ לְנָחָשׁ תִּקַּח בְּיָדֶךָ: וְאָמַרְתָּ אֵלָיו יְהֹוָה אֱלֹהֵי הָעִבְרִים שְׁלָחַנִי אֵלֶיךָ לֵאמֹר שַׁלַּח אֶת־עַמִּי וְיַעַבְדֻנִי בַּמִּדְבָּר וְהִנֵּה לֹא־שָׁמַעְתָּ עַד־כֹּה:

And יהוה said to Moses, "Pharaoh is stubborn; he refuses to let the people go. Go to Pharaoh in the morning, as he is coming out to the water, and station yourself before him at the edge of the Nile, taking with you the rod that turned into a snake. And say to him, 'יהוה, the God of the Hebrews, sent me to you to say, "Let My people go that they may worship Me in the wilderness." But you have paid no heed until now.'"

Exodus 7:21

וְהַדָּגָה אֲשֶׁר־בַּיְאֹר מֵתָה וַיִּבְאַשׁ הַיְאֹר וְלֹא־יָכְלוּ מִצְרַיִם לִשְׁתּוֹת מַיִם מִן־הַיְאֹר וַיְהִי הַדָּם בְּכָל־אֶרֶץ מִצְרָיִם:

and the fish in the Nile died. The Nile stank so that the Egyptians could not drink water from the Nile; and there was blood throughout the land of Egypt.

Exodus 7:27-28

וְאִם־מָאֵן אַתָּה לְשַׁלֵּחַ הִנֵּה אָנֹכִי נֹגֵף אֶת־כָּל־גְּבוּלְךָ בַּצְפַרְדְּעִים: וְשָׁרַץ הַיְאֹר צְפַרְדְּעִים וְעָלוּ וּבָאוּ בְּבֵיתֶךָ וּבַחֲדַר מִשְׁכָּבְךָ וְעַל־מִטָּתֶךָ וּבְבֵית עֲבָדֶיךָ וּבְעַמֶּךָ וּבְתַנּוּרֶיךָ וּבְמִשְׁאֲרוֹתֶיךָ:

If you refuse to let them go, then I will plague your whole country with frogs. The Nile shall swarm with frogs, and they shall come up and enter your palace, your bedchamber and your bed, the houses of your courtiers and your people, and your ovens and your kneading bowls.

Exodus 8:10

וַיִּצְבְּרוּ אֹתָם חֳמָרִם חֳמָרִם וַתִּבְאַשׁ הָאָרֶץ:

And they piled [the frogs] up in heaps, till the land stank.

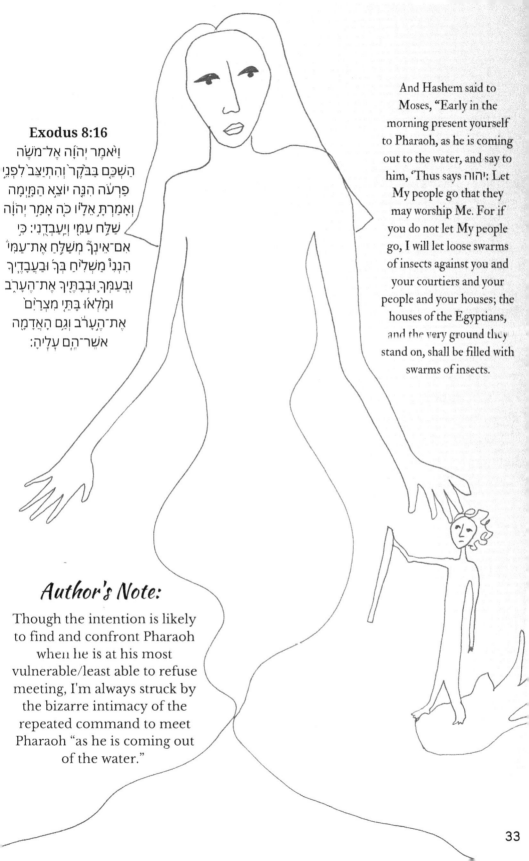

Exodus 8:16

וַיֹּ֨אמֶר יְהֹוָ֜ה אֶל־מֹשֶׁ֗ה
הַשְׁכֵּ֤ם בַּבֹּ֙קֶר֙ וְהִתְיַצֵּב֙ לִפְנֵ֣י
פַרְעֹ֔ה הִנֵּ֖ה יוֹצֵ֣א הַמָּ֑יְמָה
וְאָמַרְתָּ֣ אֵלָ֗יו כֹּ֚ה אָמַ֣ר יְהֹוָ֔ה
שַׁלַּ֥ח עַמִּ֖י וְיַֽעַבְדֻֽנִי: כִּ֣י
אִם־אֵֽינְךָ֮ מְשַׁלֵּ֣חַ אֶת־עַמִּי֒
הִנְנִי֩ מַשְׁלִ֨יחַ בְּךָ֜ וּבַעֲבָדֶ֗יךָ
וּֽבְעַמְּךָ֙ וּבְבָתֶּ֔יךָ אֶת־הֶ֣עָרֹ֑ב
וּמָ֨לְא֜וּ בָּתֵּ֤י מִצְרַ֙יִם֙
אֶת־הֶ֣עָרֹ֔ב וְגַ֥ם הָאֲדָמָ֖ה
אֲשֶׁר־הֵ֥ם עָלֶֽיהָ:

And Hashem said to Moses, "Early in the morning present yourself to Pharaoh, as he is coming out to the water, and say to him, 'Thus says יהוה: Let My people go that they may worship Me. For if you do not let My people go, I will let loose swarms of insects against you and your courtiers and your people and your houses; the houses of the Egyptians, and the very ground they stand on, shall be filled with swarms of insects.

Author's Note:

Though the intention is likely to find and confront Pharaoh when he is at his most vulnerable/least able to refuse meeting, I'm always struck by the bizarre intimacy of the repeated command to meet Pharaoh "as he is coming out of the water."

33

Bo

I sat bleeding free
in the neverending light,
and I was surrounded by people
still like shadows and I was surrounded
by men curled about themselves like crimson
question marks and at my feet there was a carcass
and at my feet there was a pool of blood and so I took
this covenant, *dam shehanefesh yotza bo* I took it in my
palms, took blood and hyssop and painted out a warning I
painted out a promise and standing beneath a dripping lintel I
watched,

as you took each bleeding
question mark of a man and
kissed him so sweetly, so gently
held each bleeding body in a sea of
light thick as tightly-woven thread and
sharp with the smell of copper. you may
have forgotten that I was not a statue, that
I stood before you in the light, my dress white
and stained and perfect, a brush of hyssop dangling
from my fingers—

can you see me now.
I wade ankle deep through
the blood. it fills the courtyard
and we stink of death and life and
you promised us, you promised us, you
promised us to come closer. look down at
me, wallowing in my blood so pitifully and so
perfectly. tell me in my blood, I will live. tell me
in spite of my blood, I will live.

Shemot Rabbah 14:3

הֲדָא הוּא דְכְתִיב: וּלְכָל בְּנֵי יִשְׂרָאֵל הָיָה
אוֹר וְגוֹ', בְּאֶרֶץ גֹּשֶׁן לֹא נֶאֱמַר אֶלָּא
בְּמוֹשְׁבֹתָם, שֶׁכָּל מָקוֹם שֶׁהָיָה יְהוּדִי נִכְנָס
הָיָה אוֹר נִכְנַס...

And [with regard to the plague of darkness] it's written, "but all the people of Israel enjoyed light in their dwellings." It didn't say "in the land of Goshen," but rather "in their dwellings," to teach that any place a Jew entered, light would enter...

Exodus 12:22

וּלְקַחְתֶּם אֲגֻדַּת אֵזוֹב וּטְבַלְתֶּם בַּדָּם אֲשֶׁר־בַּסַּף
וְהִגַּעְתֶּם אֶל־הַמַּשְׁקוֹף וְאֶל־שְׁתֵּי הַמְּזוּזֹת מִן־הַדָּם
אֲשֶׁר בַּסָּף וְאַתֶּם לֹא תֵצְאוּ אִישׁ מִפֶּתַח־בֵּיתוֹ
עַד־בֹּקֶר:

Take a bunch of hyssop, dip it in the blood that is in the basin, and apply some of the blood that is in the basin to the lintel and to the two doorposts. None of you shall go outside the door of your house until morning.

Ezekiel 16:5-6

לֹא־חָסָה עָלַיִךְ עַיִן לַעֲשׂוֹת לָךְ אַחַת מֵאֵלֶּה לְחֻמְלָה עָלָיִךְ וַתֻּשְׁלְכִי אֶל־פְּנֵי הַשָּׂדֶה
בְּגֹעַל נַפְשֵׁךְ בְּיוֹם הֻלֶּדֶת אֹתָךְ: וָאֶעֱבֹר עָלַיִךְ וָאֶרְאֵךְ מִתְבּוֹסֶסֶת בְּדָמָיִךְ וָאֹמַר לָךְ
בְּדָמַיִךְ חֲיִי וָאֹמַר לָךְ בְּדָמַיִךְ חֲיִי:

No one pitied you enough to do any one of these things for you out of compassion for you; on the day you were born, you were left lying, rejected, in the open field. When I passed by you and saw you wallowing in your blood, I said to you: "Live in spite of your blood." Yea, I said to you: "Live in spite of your blood."

Pirkei DeRabbi Eliezer 29:11

And they [the Israelites] took the blood of circumcision and the blood of the Paschal lamb, and they put it on the lintel of their homes. And when the Holy Blessed One passed over to plague the Egyptians and saw the covenant blood and the Paschal blood, They were filled with mercy for the Israelites, as it is said, "And when I passed by you and saw you wallowing in your blood, and I said to you, in your bloods [plural] live." (Ezekiel 16:7)

Pesachim 65b
Rabbi Yehuda said to the Rabbis: ... why did they plug the drains of the Temple courtyard [on Passover eve]?

They said to him: It is praiseworthy of the sons of Aaron (the priests) to walk in blood up to their ankles.

Bekhor Shor, Genesis 17:11:1
"And it will be a sign of the covenant between Me and you." A symbol and a sign that I am the Master and you are my servant...And since the Holy One, Blessed be They, commanded men and not women, we learn that the place of manhood was where the Holy One, Blessed be They, commanded to seal the covenant. And the blood of niddah [menstrual blood] that women guard, and tell their openings to their husbands, this is to them the blood of the covenant (*dam brit*).

Midrash Tanchuma, Metzora 18
Our Rabbis said: When Israel was in Egypt, the women did not menstruate because the fear of Egypt was upon them.

Nizzahon Vetus (13th century, Germany)
"And they shall take of the blood" [Exod. 12:7] refers to three drops: "Put it on the lintel" refers to one, "and on the two side-posts" refers to two more. Thus the passage refers to three types of blood: [the blood of the lamb], of circumcision, and of the menstruant woman.

Shemot Rabbah 19:5
The Holy One Blessed Be They said: If you are not circumcised, you cannot eat [the passover sacrifice]... They immediately circumcised themselves, and the blood of the passover sacrifice mingled with the blood from the circumcision, and The Holy One Blessed Be They passed over and held each one and kissed it and blessed it, as it says, "And when I passed by thee, and saw thee wallowing in thy blood, I said unto thee: In thy blood, live; yea, I said unto thee: In thy blood, live!" (Ezekiel 16:6)

Beshallach

this is my God and I will
revere Them this one the one
to whom I am pointing right
pinky extended impertinently just
me and the young boy beside me the
young man at his shoulder the little
boy at his feet our heads are still dusty
from the fields our toes still spread like
roots and our mothers' arms still feel like
rocks of milk and honey, rocks of
anointment, like an inescapable embrace,
like God's arms,
and we can still taste that honey on
our tongues. this is my God I
say, this God standing before me, blowing
waves into paths of spun glass and freezing
a dome above our heads, the cloud and the
fire and the song—*this* is our God, we say,
outlining Their shape with our pinkies, carving
an image for the mothers at our backs.
you are our God,
we remember your face.

Exodus 14:21-22

וַיֵּ֨ט מֹשֶׁ֣ה אֶת־יָדוֹ֮ עַל־הַיָּם֒ וַיּ֣וֹלֶךְ יְהֹוָ֣ה | אֶת־הַ֠יָּ֠ם בְּר֨וּחַ קָדִ֤ים עַזָּה֙ כׇּל־הַלַּ֔יְלָה וַיָּ֥שֶׂם אֶת־הַיָּ֖ם לֶחָרָבָ֑ה וַיִּבָּקְע֖וּ הַמָּֽיִם: וַיָּבֹ֧אוּ בְנֵֽי־יִשְׂרָאֵ֛ל בְּת֥וֹךְ הַיָּ֖ם בַּיַּבָּשָׁ֑ה וְהַמַּ֤יִם לָהֶם֙ חוֹמָ֔ה מִֽימִינָ֖ם וּמִשְּׂמֹאלָֽם:

Then Moses held out his arm over the sea and
Hashem drove back the sea with a strong east wind
all that night, and turned the sea into dry ground.
The waters were split, and the Israelites went into
the sea on dry ground, the waters forming a wall
for them on their right and on their left.

Exodus 15:1-2

אָ֣ז יָשִֽׁיר־מֹשֶׁה֩ וּבְנֵ֨י יִשְׂרָאֵ֜ל אֶת־הַשִּׁירָ֤ה הַזֹּאת֙ לַֽיהֹוָ֔ה וַיֹּאמְר֖וּ לֵאמֹ֑ר אָשִׁ֤ירָה לַֽיהֹוָה֙ כִּֽי־גָאֹ֣ה גָּאָ֔ה ס֥וּס וְרֹכְב֖וֹ רָמָ֥ה בַיָּֽם: עׇזִּ֤י וְזִמְרָת֙ יָ֔הּ וַֽיְהִי־לִ֖י לִֽישׁוּעָ֑ה זֶ֤ה אֵלִי֙ וְאַנְוֵ֔הוּ אֱלֹהֵ֥י אָבִ֖י וַאֲרֹמְמֶֽנְהוּ:

Then Moses and the
Israelites sang this song to
God. They said:
I will sing to God for They
have triumphed gloriously;
Horse and rider They have
hurled into the sea.
God is my strength and
might;
They are become my
deliverance.
This is my God and I will
glorify Them;
The God of my father, and I
will exalt Them.

Mekhilta d'Rabbi Yishmael 14:16:1
"And you, raise your staff": Ten miracles were performed for Israel at the sea: The waters were split and became like a dome, viz. (Habakkuk 3:14) "You split (the sea) for his tribes; the summit of its scattering raged to scatter me"...they became like a wall, viz. (Ibid.) "the waves stood up as a wall"...They froze the sea for them and it became like vessels of glass, viz. (Exodus 15:8) "The depths froze in the midst of the sea."

**Rashi
Exodus
15:2**
THIS IS
MY GOD–
In Their
glory did
They reveal
Themself to
the people
and they
pointed to
Them–as it
were–with
the finger,
exclaiming,
"This is my
God!" (Shir
HaShirim
Rabbah 3:15)

Shemot Rabbah 1:12

And when these women would become pregnant, they would come back to their homes, and then they would go and give birth in the field under the apple tree, as it is stated: "Under the apple tree I awakened you; there your mother was in travail with you; there was she in travail and brought you forth" (Song of Songs 8:5). And the Holy One, Blessed be They, would clean and prepare the newborns, just as a midwife prepares the newborn, as it is stated: "And as for your birth, on the day you were born, your navel was not cut nor were you washed with water for cleansing..." (Ezekiel 16:4). And then, They would gather for them two round stones from the field and the babies would nurse from that which would flow out of them: one with oil and one with honey, as it is stated: "And They would suckle them with honey from a crag and oil from a flinty rock" (Deuteronomy 32:13). And once the Egyptians would notice the babies, they would come to kill them. But a miracle would occur and they would be absorbed by the earth... After the Egyptians would leave, the babies would emerge and exit the ground like grass of the field, as it is stated: "I caused you to increase even as the growth of the field" (Ezekiel 16:7). And once the babies would grow, they would come like many flocks of sheep to their homes, as it is stated: "And you did increase and grow up and you came with excellent beauty [*ba'adi adayim*]" (Ezekiel 16:7)...read it as: *be'edrei adarim*, meaning: as many flocks. And when the Holy One, Blessed be They, revealed Themself at the Red Sea, these children recognized Them first, as it is stated: "This is my God, and I will glorify Them" (Exodus 15:2).

The song of dry land, of timbrels
and dance, must always follow
another, older song.

Song of fear and faith
clouds and fire behind, water ahead—
who is like you—
The waves rise, choking on salt—
who is like you?
I will sing.
Bitter sea to sweet water.

Exodus 14:19-22

וַיִּסַּ֞ע מַלְאַ֣ךְ הָאֱלֹהִ֗ים הַהֹלֵךְ֙ לִפְנֵי֙ מַחֲנֵ֣ה יִשְׂרָאֵ֔ל וַיֵּ֖לֶךְ מֵאַחֲרֵיהֶ֑ם וַיִּסַּ֞ע עַמּ֤וּד הֶֽעָנָן֙ מִפְּנֵיהֶ֔ם וַֽיַּעֲמֹ֖ד מֵאַחֲרֵיהֶֽם: וַיָּבֹ֞א בֵּ֣ין | מַחֲנֵ֣ה מִצְרַ֗יִם וּבֵין֙ מַחֲנֵ֣ה יִשְׂרָאֵ֔ל וַיְהִ֤י הֶֽעָנָן֙ וְהַחֹ֔שֶׁךְ וַיָּ֖אֶר אֶת־הַלָּ֑יְלָה וְלֹא־קָרַ֥ב זֶ֛ה אֶל־זֶ֖ה כָּל־הַלָּֽיְלָה: וַיֵּ֨ט מֹשֶׁ֣ה אֶת־יָדוֹ֘ עַל־הַיָּם֒ וַיּ֣וֹלֶךְ יְהֹוָ֣ה | אֶת־הַ֠יָּ֠ם בְּר֨וּחַ קָדִ֤ים עַזָּה֙ כָּל־הַלַּ֔יְלָה וַיָּ֥שֶׂם אֶת־הַיָּ֖ם לֶחָרָבָ֑ה וַיִּבָּקְע֖וּ הַמָּֽיִם: וַיָּבֹ֧אוּ בְנֵֽי־יִשְׂרָאֵ֛ל בְּת֥וֹךְ הַיָּ֖ם בַּיַּבָּשָׁ֑ה וְהַמַּ֤יִם לָהֶם֙ חוֹמָ֔ה מִֽימִינָ֖ם וּמִשְּׂמֹאלָֽם:

The messenger of God, who had been going ahead of the Israelite army, now moved and followed behind them; and the pillar of cloud shifted from in front of them and took up a place behind them, and it came between the army of the Egyptians and the army of Israel. Thus there was the cloud with the darkness, and it cast a spell upon the night, so that the one could not come near the other all through the night. Then Moses held out his arm over the sea and God drove back the sea with a strong east wind all that night, and turned the sea into dry ground. The waters were split, and the Israelites went into the sea on dry ground, the waters forming a wall for them on their right and on their left.

Bamidbar Rabbah 13:4

Rabbi Yehudah bar Ilai said: When Israel was at the sea, the tribes were arguing with each other. One tribe said: 'I will go down first [into the sea]', and the other tribe said 'I will go down first.' Nachshon jumped first into the waves of the sea and went down, and on him David said, "Deliver me, O God, for the waters have reached my neck."

we began singing before we
even reached the shore, began
singing as the walls of water
crashed down behind us while we
walked on dry and silty ground, we
were limned by sea spray and the
scattered light glancing off our
tambourines and swollen crystal
bellies. *shiru lahashem*, we tapped
out worship with our dancing feet.
ki gaoh ga'ah they sang, jostling in
our stomachs. we had prepared for
this moment, had strode to the faint
clinging of bells from the moment we'd
left Egypt. we had prepared for this,
ecstatic movement and clashing voices as our
toes hit the sand and their corpses washed
up by our feet. our joy & relief thrummed
out the rhythm of free, free, free, free,
horse and rider They have hurled into the sea.

Mekhilta d'Rabbi Yishmael 15:20:2
WITH TIMBRELS AND WITH
DANCES — The righteous women in that
generation were confident that God would
perform miracles for them and they
accordingly had brought timbrels with them
from Egypt.

Yitro

a mountain overturned
sheets spread smooth rippling
luxurious on a sturdy frame
a mountain overturned and all
in fire, all in ashes,
a revelation or a grave—
we are trembling in terror/awe.

the only thing you cannot create
is our terror/awe;

you created the world to
finally see your reflection
and when you find the
waters still & opaque you
think, maybe I will un-create,
maybe then I can excuse this
longing, this loneness.

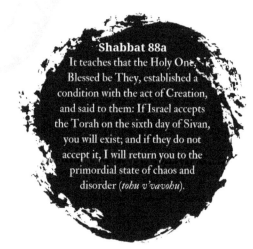

Shabbat 88a
"And they stood at the bottom of the mountain."
(Exodus 19:17) — Rabbi Avdimi the son of
Chama the son of Chasa said, "This teaches that
the Holy One, Blessed be They, held the
mountain over them like a barrel and said, 'If
you accept the Torah, it is good. And if not, here
shall be your graves.'"

Shabbat 88a
It teaches that the Holy One,
Blessed be They, established a
condition with the act of Creation,
and said to them: If Israel accepts
the Torah on the sixth day of Sivan,
you will exist; and if they do not
accept it, I will return you to the
primordial state of chaos and
disorder (*tohu v'vavohu*).

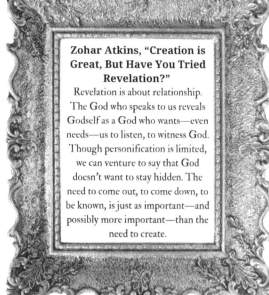

Yalkut Shimoni on Torah 855:3
And Rabbi Hanina said: Everything is in
the hands of Heaven, except for fear of
Heaven. Man has free will to serve God or
not, as it is stated: "And now Israel, what
does the Lord your God ask of you other
than to fear the Lord your God, to walk in
all of His ways, to love Him and to serve
the Lord your God with all your heart and
with all your soul" (Deuteronomy 10:12).

**Zohar Atkins, "Creation is
Great, But Have You Tried
Revelation?"**
Revelation is about relationship.
The God who speaks to us reveals
Godself as a God who wants—even
needs—us to listen, to witness God.
Though personification is limited,
we can venture to say that God
doesn't want to stay hidden. The
need to come out, to come down, to
be known, is just as important—and
possibly more important—than the
need to create.

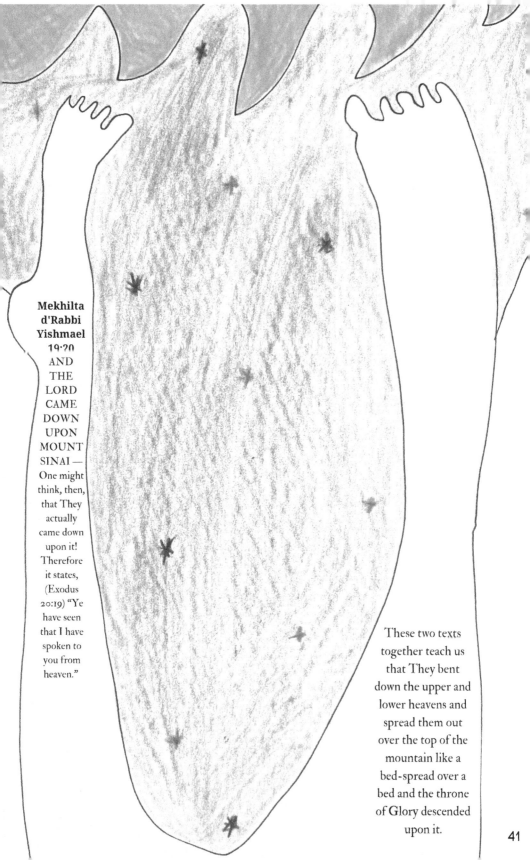

Mekhilta d'Rabbi Yishmael 19:20
AND THE LORD CAME DOWN UPON MOUNT SINAI — One might think, then, that They actually came down upon it! Therefore it states, (Exodus 20:19) "Ye have seen that I have spoken to you from heaven."

These two texts together teach us that They bent down the upper and lower heavens and spread them out over the top of the mountain like a bed-spread over a bed and the throne of Glory descended upon it.

the mountain was consumed
in fire God's words were
fire the parchment was
fire the law was
fire the thread was
fire the angels gathered eager thronging
waiting at its base were all
in fire and Moshe's face,
bright, intoxicated with Torah,
all in fire, and it was beautiful and
it hurt to touch and we can only step
back because we have not, yet,
learned how to sit in weave around learn amidst
the fire and

       it is still beautiful and untouchable
and, we are in love and we are
afraid and, we have not yet learned
that both love & Torah should set us on
fire.

and Ben Azzai was there too,
you know—
sat small and near invisible at
the mountain's base, and he almost—
just barely—
brushed Moshe's leg as the prophet
plodded past, heavy and alight,
and as b'nei yisrael retreated he
sat still and joyful at the mountain's
base, stringing together words of
Torah, and the words were sweet,
and the voices were still,
and he was all in fire.

> **Midrash Tanchuma, Yitro 16:2**
> You find that when the Holy One, blessed
> be He, gave the Torah, it was entirely of
> fire, as it is said: At His right hand was a
> fiery law unto them (Deut. 33:2). Our sages
> stated: The law was of fire, the parchment
> was of fire, its writings were of fire, the
> thread was of fire, as it is said: At Their
> right hand was a fiery law. The face of the
> agent (Moses) became fiery, as is said: And
> they were afraid to come nigh him (Exod.
> 34:30). The angels who descended with it
> were of fire, as it is said: Who makes winds
> Thy messengers (Ps. 104:4). The mountain
> burned with fire (Deut. 4:11), and it was
> given within a fire consuming fire, as it is
> said: For the Lord thy God is a devouring
> fire (ibid. 4:24). And upon the earth They
> made thee to see Their great fire (ibid., v.
> 36). The Divine Word also came forth from
> the midst of fire. When they beheld the
> lightning and the burning letters, the Holy
> One, blessed be They, said to them: Do not
> imagine that they have much power, and
> They began to recite the words I am the
> Lord thy God. Thou shalt have no other
> gods (Exod. 20:2).

> **Shir HaShirim Rabbah 1:10**
> Ben Azzai was sitting and expounding, and fire was blazing around
> him. They [his disciples] came and told Rabbi Akiva, "Rabbi Ben
> Azzai is sitting and expounding, and fire is blazing around him."
> [Akiva] went to him and said, "I heard that you were sitting and
> expounding, and fire was blazing around you!" [Ben Azzai]
> replied, "Yes." [Akiva] said to him, "Perhaps you are engaged in
> the chambers of the Chariot [the secrets of Ezekiel's vision of the
> Chariot]?!" [Ben Azzai] replied, "No, I am sitting and stringing
> words of Torah, from Torah to the Prophets, and from Prophets
> to the Writings, and the words are as joyous as on the day they were
> given from Sinai, and as sweet (sonorous, fragrant) as the essence
> [ikar] of what was given. And the essence that was given [that day]
> on Sinai, were they not [originally] given in fire?!" and the
> mountain burned with fire (Deut. 4:11).

> **Exodus 20:15**
> וְכָל־הָעָם רֹאִים אֶת־הַקּוֹלֹת וְאֶת־הַלַּפִּידִם וְאֵת קוֹל הַשֹּׁפָר
> וְאֶת־הָהָר עָשֵׁן וַיַּרְא הָעָם וַיָּנֻעוּ וַיַּעַמְדוּ מֵרָחֹק:
> All the people witnessed the thunder and lightning, the blare
> of the horn and the mountain smoking; and when the people
> saw it, they fell back and stood at a distance.

Horns blast through the thick cloud
of ozone. Lightning strikes.
My people are trembling.
Sinai blazes, with furnace smoke
the mountain shakes.

I, I am God who freed you
I make light and darkness
bless you and keep you.
I am God
I am
I.

Zera Kodesh (R Horowitz), 2:40

ששמעתי מן פי אדמו"ר מרימנאב מהר"מ
ז"ל על פסוק אחת דיבר אלקים וכו' שאפשר
שלא שמענו מפי הקב"ה רק אות א' דאנכי

I heard from the mouth of the Master
from Rimanov, our teacher Rabbi
Mendel, may his memory be for a
blessing, about the verse "God spoke
one..." [Psalms 62:12] that it is possible
that we only heard from the mouth of
the Holy Blessed One the letter aleph
from the word anochi, I

Mishpatim

na'aseh v'nishmah,

an angel for each man
to rest a crown on his
head, proudly,

an angel for each man
to rest a second crown
on his brow and it will
droop forward, obscuring
his eyes; his vision will
be filled with gold and he
will not see the woman standing
before him, the woman standing
before him with the Torah on
her mouth and their child in her
arms, her head bowed and
bare.

> **Exodus 24:7**
> וַיִּקַּח סֵפֶר הַבְּרִית וַיִּקְרָא בְּאָזְנֵי הָעָם וַיֹּאמְרוּ כֹּל
> אֲשֶׁר־דִּבֶּר יְהוָה נַעֲשֶׂה וְנִשְׁמָע:
> Then [Moshe] took the record of the
> covenant and read it aloud to the people. And
> they said, "All that Hashem has spoken we
> will do and we will hear!"

> **Shabbat 88a**
> Rabbi Simai taught: When Israel accorded precedence to the declaration "We will
> do" over the declaration "We will hear," 600,000 ministering angels came and tied
> two crowns to each and every member of the Jewish people, one corresponding to
> "We will do" and one corresponding to "We will hear."

Author's Note:

The midrash says ministering angels came and tied two crowns "to every member of the Jewish people." 600,000 angels came. 600,000 is the number of Israelite men above the age of twenty.

Terumah

and this is how much I love you, she says—enough to retract myself from the Heavens, to take my expansiveness and make it presence, to take my dwelling and make it singular—here, between the two keruvim, I alight on the ark and I will speak to you beneath the shelter of their wings, their faces almost touching but not quite, my presence almost finite but never just, your face alight and my voice shaking the flaps of this goat-hair tent. this is how much I love you—enough to shrink myself, momentarily. to slip between the hairsbreadth dividing these angels' lips. to gird myself in goats' hair and whisper, through the shadows of seven soft flickering lights.

build me a home and paint it blue. I will come to you.

וְהָי֣וּ הַכְּרֻבִים֩ פֹּרְשֵׂ֨י כְנָפַ֜יִם לְמַ֗עְלָה סֹכְכִ֤ים בְּכַנְפֵיהֶם֙ עַל־הַכַּפֹּ֔רֶת
וּפְנֵיהֶ֖ם אִ֣ישׁ אֶל־אָחִ֑יו אֶל־הַכַּפֹּ֔רֶת יִהְי֖וּ פְּנֵ֥י הַכְּרֻבִֽים׃

The cherubim shall have their wings spread out above, shielding the cover with their wings. They shall confront each other, the faces of the cherubim being turned toward the cover.

we face each other we face each other we face each other wings almost, barely, touching, heads bowed wings reaching, earnestly, above and we will not look at you; we refuse to be worshiped. sometimes we will be looking just above you, beyond you, towards a bare and brilliant hill— mostly, we will face each other. wings stretching heads bowed, almost, as if in mourning, we strive for the holy but are bound to this earth, this ark, each other. perhaps we will look down and find it was holy, always, too—perhaps our gaze will skip over yours for the briefest moment as we turn from the hill, and we will see your naked yearning and turn away from it. we will face each other, the space of a finger, a kiss, between us. we cannot help you. we are not God, that you should worship us. only gold desperately alive, shading the Torah with every chiseled feather.

Sforno on Exodus 25:20

The reason why the Torah continues in describing these cherubs as facing the lid of the Ark, i.e. looking downwards whereas their wings are spread upwards, is a reminder that although inspiration originates in heaven, understanding of G'd and how They work can only come by studying what They do in our material, "lower" part of Their universe. The ideal means of unraveling the meaning of G'd's actions is through Their revealed word, the Torah, of which the Ark has become the repository.

Chizkuni on Exodus 25:20

Seeing, however, that they faced each other, is clear proof that they had no interest in any onlooker. Furthermore, though their wings were pointing upwards, their faces were looking down at the lid, i.e. the space from which G-d's words would emanate to Moses, and the area in which the Torah was kept. The most important proof that they were not meant to be worshiped by anyone, is the fact that they were in a place that was inaccessible to the people on pain of death. Their function therefore was merely to be servants of G-d rather than Their competitors, just as the cherubs in Isaiah 6:2 were perceived as G-d's servants standing in attendance before G-d's throne.

Bava Batra 99a

How were the cherubs standing? One rabbi says: Their faces were turned one toward the other. And one says: Their faces were turned toward the House, i.e., the Sanctuary. But according to the one who says that their faces were turned one toward the other, isn't it written: "And their faces were toward the House" (II Chronicles 3:13)? This is not difficult: Here, when it states that the cherubs faced each other, it was when the Jewish people do the will of God. There, when it says they faced the Sanctuary, was when the Jewish people do not do the will of God.

In the wilderness
spiced smoke surrounds
the sanctuary. Past
the twisted linen
lies its billowing court.
inside the goat-hair curtain,
defence against the desert dust,
through blue, purple, crimson and gold
is holy space.

Through the veil of thought
words fill the wooden ark.
Inside the words
is me.

Exodus 25:8-9

וְעָשׂוּ לִי מִקְדָּשׁ וְשָׁכַנְתִּי בְּתוֹכָם:
כְּכֹל אֲשֶׁר אֲנִי מַרְאֶה אוֹתְךָ אֵת תַּבְנִית הַמִּשְׁכָּן וְאֵת תַּבְנִית
כָּל־כֵּלָיו וְכֵן תַּעֲשׂוּ:

And let them make Me a sanctuary that I may dwell
among them.
Exactly as I show you—the pattern of the Tabernacle and
the pattern of all its furnishings—so shall you make it.

Tetzaveh

make atonement with my
tattered sweater, these self-
ripped jeans, each hastily-
wrapped scarf. give them
a vision of patterned skirts
hairy legs dangling tzitzis
scuffed boots and let them
be forgiven. let me wear what
feels holy and be forgiven.
when I am dressed, thoughtfully,
as my fullest self—I am intricate
& divine. on my forehead, along
the brim of a hat or the tassel
of a drooping scarf, it reads
holy to hashem. every day that
I wake up, I prepare myself to
serve you.

Exodus 28:2
וְעָשִׂ֛יתָ בִגְדֵי־קֹ֥דֶשׁ לְאַהֲרֹ֖ן אָחִ֑יךָ לְכָב֖וֹד
וּלְתִפְאָֽרֶת:
Make sacral vestments for your brother
Aaron, for dignity and adornment.

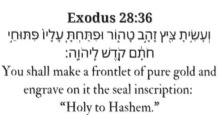

Exodus 28:36
וְעָשִׂ֥יתָ צִּ֖יץ זָהָ֣ב טָה֑וֹר וּפִתַּחְתָּ֤ עָלָיו֙ פִּתּוּחֵ֣י
חֹתָ֔ם קֹ֖דֶשׁ לַֽיהֹוָֽה:
You shall make a frontlet of pure gold and
engrave on it the seal inscription:
"Holy to Hashem."

Exodus 28:38
וְהָיָה֮ עַל־מֵ֣צַח אַהֲרֹן֒ וְנָשָׂ֨א אַהֲרֹ֜ן אֶת־עֲוֺ֣ן הַקֳּדָשִׁ֗ים אֲשֶׁ֤ר יַקְדִּ֙ישׁוּ֙ בְּנֵ֣י יִשְׂרָאֵ֔ל לְכָֽל־מַתְּנֹ֖ת קׇדְשֵׁיהֶ֑ם וְהָיָ֤ה
עַל־מִצְחוֹ֙ תָּמִ֔יד לְרָצ֥וֹן לָהֶ֖ם לִפְנֵ֥י יְהֹוָֽה:
It shall be on Aaron's forehead, that Aaron may take away any sin arising from the holy things that the
Israelites consecrate, from any of their sacred donations; it shall be on his forehead at all times, to win
acceptance for them before Hashem.

Ilana Kurshan, Parshat Tetzaveh: "Dress and Redress"

Clothing, then, is not just functional and ornamental; it also plays a spiritual role, reconciling between humanity and God...The Talmud (Zevachim 17b) teaches that the priest is not a priest unless he is wearing his sacred vestments, based on a verse from our parsha: "And you shall gird Aaron and his son with sashes, and so they shall have the priesthood on them at all time" (29:9). The rabbis conclude that "when their vestments are upon them, the priesthood is upon them; but if their vestments are not on them, the priesthood is not on them." A priest could not just roll out of bed and serve in the Temple; the act of getting dressed transformed him from an ordinary person into a functionary engaged in divine service.

[Clothes] are about the care we take to transform ourselves in the morning from a creature asleep to a human being engaged in divine service. When we sleep we are like animals – our souls, that part of the divine that sets us apart from other creatures, are entrusted to God. When we wake, our souls are restored to our bodies and we become once again not just creatures of nature, but also individuals with culture and inner spiritual lives. By getting dressed, we symbolize that transformation.

HOLY

50

Ki Tissa

when I was little,
Moshe,
I thought you were
mad, childish, breaking
your favorite toy rather
than sharing it,
and I didn't know–

that you were angry and
devastated and
fearful and
defiant—

that you clasped Hashem's
coat till it nearly tore,
that before you'd had
the chance even to
see Them pass before you
Their cloak was clutched
in your hands cloth bruising
your fingers, pleading,
breathlessly,
until They said
hanikha li
and you said no,

that you'd rather be a
name blotted from the
book than a fresh page
in a new sefer,

and that when you broke
our Torah it was with fury
and it was with fear and
it was with love,

because it wasn't for nothing that
you'd held G-d so long in
your hands.

the stones didn't slip
through your fingers—
you cast them at our
feet, shattered and lovely,
and we saw a wisp of thread
holding up the *samekh* in
mid-air (small and ragged
as though torn) and you
said,

look what I have done for you.

Berakhot 32a
The phrase: Let Me be,
teaches that Moses grabbed
the Holy One, Blessed be
They, as a person who grabs
his friend by his garment
would, and he said before
Them: Master of the
Universe, I will not leave You
be until You forgive and
pardon them.

Exodus 32:19
וַיְהִי כַּאֲשֶׁר קָרַב אֶל־הַמַּחֲנֶה
וַיַּרְא אֶת־הָעֵגֶל וּמְחֹלֹת
וַיִּחַר־אַף מֹשֶׁה וַיַּשְׁלֵךְ מִיָּדוֹ
אֶת־הַלֻּחֹת וַיְשַׁבֵּר אֹתָם תַּחַת
הָהָר׃
As soon as Moses came near
the camp and saw the calf
and the dancing, he became
enraged; and he hurled the
tablets from his hands and
shattered them at the foot
of the mountain.

Exodus 32:7-10
וַיְדַבֵּר יְהוָה אֶל־מֹשֶׁה לֶךְ־רֵד כִּי שִׁחֵת עַמְּךָ אֲשֶׁר הֶעֱלֵיתָ מֵאֶרֶץ מִצְרָיִם: סָרוּ מַהֵר
מִן־הַדֶּרֶךְ אֲשֶׁר צִוִּיתִם עָשׂוּ לָהֶם עֵגֶל מַסֵּכָה וַיִּשְׁתַּחֲווּ־לוֹ וַיִּזְבְּחוּ־לוֹ וַיֹּאמְרוּ אֵלֶּה
אֱלֹהֶיךָ יִשְׂרָאֵל אֲשֶׁר הֶעֱלוּךָ מֵאֶרֶץ מִצְרָיִם: וַיֹּאמֶר יְהוָה אֶל־מֹשֶׁה רָאִיתִי
אֶת־הָעָם הַזֶּה וְהִנֵּה עַם־קְשֵׁה־עֹרֶף הוּא: וְעַתָּה הַנִּיחָה לִּי וְיִחַר־אַפִּי בָהֶם וַאֲכַלֵּם
וְאֶעֱשֶׂה אוֹתְךָ לְגוֹי גָּדוֹל:
Hashem spoke to Moses, "Hurry down, for your people, whom you brought
out of the land of Egypt, have acted basely. They have been quick to turn
aside from the way that I enjoined upon them. They have made themselves a
molten calf and bowed low to it and sacrificed to it, saying: 'This is your god,
O Israel, who brought you out of the land of Egypt!'" Hashem further said
to Moses, "I see that this is a stiffnecked people. Now, let Me be, that My
anger may blaze forth against them and that I may destroy them, and make
of you a great nation."

Tur HaAroch on Exodus 32:19

HE SHATTERED THEM. According to the plain meaning of the text, the reason why Moses made a point of smashing the Tablets was that these Tablets which had inscribed on them that Israelites must not make a cast image of anything in heaven or on earth, would, if allowed to remain intact, serve as testimony against the people who had so grossly violated what was written upon these Tablets.

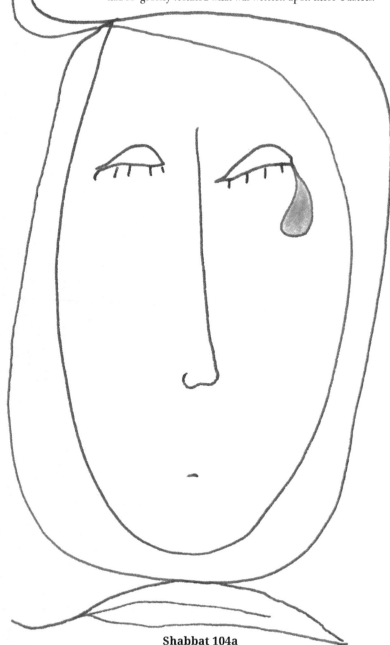

Shabbat 104a

Rav Ḥisda said: The letters *mem* and *samekh* that were in the tablets were standing miraculously. Each letter was chiseled all the way through the tablets. In that case, the segment of the tablets at the center of the samekh and final mem, letters that are completely closed, should have fallen. Miraculously, they remained in place.

hide in the cleft of the rock, my dove, and I will lay my palm on your cheek, your softly-shut eyes—you will see only my voice and my back, but this is what I meant, when I said face-to-face. me, gazing at you; you, blind and expectant.

when I lift my palm, you will be so glorious it hurts. you are too good for them and you will return to them. maybe it will hurt, that they can't look upon your face as I did. you love them and they cannot see you; you love them and they will only ever see your veil or my glory. but when I passed you, hidden in the cleft of the rock–

your eyelids fluttering, hair stirring, breath soft but eager and the faintest flush on each cheek—

I thought, maybe I have never looked at a human face before.

I thought, you were the loveliest thing I'd ever seen.

Vayakhel-Pekudei

you forced off my jewelry to
pay your penance but this
I'll give for free. remember
in Egypt, our hands burned
raw by rope eyes squint shut
against the sand and us, soft
and brilliant in the copper—

I am handsomer, I said.
I am handsomer, I say.

remember you loved me so
sweetly, and worshiped these
golden feet. remember, you
needed no instruction.

you've built your worship
like a woman's body and
kept me out of it.

I'll sit here spinning the
wool off each small & bleating
goat, watch your elaborate
dance in this copper reflection,
glinting golden in the sunlight–

and if I miss a moment of it,
then no matter. you don't need
to show me. I already know how
it feels, to be purified in blood.

Pirkei DeRabbi Eliezer 45:4
Aaron argued with himself, saying: If I say to Israel, Give ye to me gold and silver, they will bring it immediately; but behold I will say to them, Give ye to me the earrings of your wives, and of your sons, and forthwith the matter will fail, as it is said, "And Aaron said to them, Break off the golden rings etc." (Ex. 32:2). The women heard (this), but they were unwilling to give their earrings to their husbands; instead they replied: Ye desire to make a graven image and a molten image without any power in it to deliver.

Exodus 35:22
וַיָּבֹאוּ הָאֲנָשִׁים עַל־הַנָּשִׁים כֹּל ׀ נְדִיב לֵב הֵבִיאוּ חָח וָנֶזֶם וְטַבַּעַת וְכוּמָז כָּל־כְּלִי זָהָב וְכָל־אִישׁ אֲשֶׁר הֵנִיף תְּנוּפַת זָהָב לַיהוָה:
Men and women, all whose hearts moved them, all who would make an elevation offering of gold to Hashem, came bringing brooches, earrings, rings, and pendants—gold objects of all kinds.

Chizkuni on Exodus 35:22
"The men came 'upon' the women": to take away their jewelry in order to use them for building the Tabernacle, as we will read presently.

Rashi on Exodus 35:26
[AND THE WOMEN] SPUN THE GOATS' HAIR (lit., the goats) — This required extraordinary skill, for they spun it (the goats' hair) from off the backs of the goats (whilst it was still on the living animals) (Shabbat 99a).

Exodus 38:8
וַיַּעַשׂ אֵת הַכִּיּוֹר נְחֹשֶׁת וְאֵת כַּנּוֹ נְחֹשֶׁת בְּמַרְאֹת הַצֹּבְאֹת אֲשֶׁר צָבְאוּ פֶּתַח אֹהֶל מוֹעֵד:
He made the laver of copper and its stand of copper, from the mirrors of the women who performed tasks at the entrance of the Tent of Meeting.

Midrash Tanchuma, Pekudei 9

The Israelite women possessed mirrors of copper into which they used to look when they adorned themselves. Even these did they not hesitate to bring as a contribution towards the Tabernacle. Now Moses was about to reject them since they were made to pander to their vanity, but the Holy One, blessed be They, said to him, "Accept them; these are dearer to Me than all the other contributions, because through them the women reared those huge hosts in Egypt!" For when their husbands were tired through the crushing labour they used to bring them food and drink and induced them to eat. Then they would take the mirrors, and each gazed at herself in her mirror together with her husband, saying endearingly to him, "See, I am handsomer than you!" Thus they awakened their husbands' affection and subsequently became the mothers of many children, at it is said, (Song 8:5) "I awakened thy love under the apple-tree," (referring to the fields where the men worked). This is what it refers to when it states, מראות הצבאת "the mirrors of the women who reared the hosts (צבאות)"

R. Bonna Devora Haberman,
"The Yom Kippur Avoda within the Female Enclosure"

My understanding of the significance of the Avoda ritual is rooted in my association of the holy enclosures—the Tabernacle, the Temple, and, derivatively, the synagogue sanctuary—with the body of a woman... If the inner sanctuaries of the Jewish people are uterine, to them I attribute uterine functions. The cycles of daily, monthly, and festival offerings in the Tabernacle and Temple replicated the cyclical functions of the womb. Regular rites of sacrifice were performed, expiations accomplished, and blood drained...The menstrual blood flow is purification from loss of potential life, as the flow of blood in the Tabernacle is purification from sin.

Tur HaArokh on Exodus 38:8

The women, who were not normally admitted to the courtyard of the Tabernacle, and who were anxious to observe some procedures...wanted to watch the proceedings by means of the mirrors reflecting same over a distance.

Vayikra

Come closer.
Come close by blood, by fat
by smoke and slaughter.
Draw near with oil, choice flour
the smell of burnt feathers.
Don't forget salt
for the promise of the seas.
For sins, for peace
for touching death
For all these—
come close.

Rashi on Leviticus 2:13
מלח ברית [NEITHER SHALT THOU SUFFER] THE SALT OF THE COVENANT [... TO BE LACKING FROM MY MEAL OFFERING], because a covenant was established with the salt as far back as the six days of Creation when the lower waters (those of the oceans) received an assurance that they would be offered on the altar in the form of salt and also as water in the ceremony of "the libation of water" on the Feast of Tabernacles).

and now that you have
made something perfect,
let me tell you that it
will be ruined,
constantly,
that everything pure and
perfect will be soiled
and everything sacred
desacralized but
then—
hear me out—
you will come closer.

l'hakriv, bring me something
perfect and splash this
dwelling with its blood;
you'll step closer, draw
near, and my home will be
new and bloody and pure and—
hear me out—
you'll do it again.

over and over, you'll
make something perfect and
ruin it in the same breath, and
every time, you'll draw just
a step nearer. come even
closer, love—
I've grown so lonely.

Rabbi Daniel Isaacson, "Sharing a Meal with the Creator of the World"
The *mishkan* had a magnetic quality that literally attracted this impurity—the ritual and moral impurities of *tumah* and *avon*—which the Torah considered actual, physically polluting substances. Thus the latter part of our parashah, in chapters 4 and 5, lists the *hattat* and *asham korbanot* that were meant to purify and transform the effects of sin and ritual impurity, by way of blood, so that Israel could maintain the conditions necessary for the transcendent God to remain immanent.

Author's Note:

I've always been fascinated by the obsessive perfectionism of the mishkan, this idealized & precise dwelling where we commune with God, being followed immediately by Parshat Vayikra; this parsha, which details a variety of offerings, devotes a large section to the offerings made in expiation for sin. We create an image of unblemished perfection, followed immediately by the acknowledgement that this ideal will be ruptured. And yet these ruptures don't invalidate the possibility of divine perfection—they are, in fact, an opportunity for us to recommit, to draw closer.

Leviticus 8:13

וַיַּקְרֵב מֹשֶׁה אֶת־בְּנֵי אַהֲרֹן וַיַּלְבִּשֵׁם כֻּתֳּנֹת וַיַּחְגֹּר אֹתָם אַבְנֵט וַיַּחֲבֹשׁ לָהֶם מִגְבָּעוֹת כַּאֲשֶׁר צִוָּה יְהוָה אֶת־מֹשֶׁה׃

Moses then brought Aaron's sons forward, clothed them in tunics, girded them with sashes, and wound turbans upon them, as יהוה had commanded Moses.

Tzav

blood on every earlobe and wiggling big toe, our solemn faces limned in purples, blues, crimsons, light—we have spilled our blood on the stage, eager and anxious and ready. we are waiting, waiting, waiting —for the fats and flesh to catch fire, for the crowd to weep in ecstatic applause.

Exodus 28:6

וְעָשׂוּ אֶת־הָאֵפֹד זָהָב תְּכֵלֶת וְאַרְגָּמָן תּוֹלַעַת שָׁנִי וְשֵׁשׁ מָשְׁזָר מַעֲשֵׂה חֹשֵׁב׃

They shall make the ephod of gold, of blue, purple, and crimson yarns, and of fine twisted linen, worked into designs.

Leviticus 8:24

וַיַּקְרֵב אֶת־בְּנֵי אַהֲרֹן וַיִּתֵּן מֹשֶׁה מִן־הַדָּם עַל־תְּנוּךְ אָזְנָם הַיְמָנִית וְעַל־בֹּהֶן יָדָם הַיְמָנִית וְעַל־בֹּהֶן רַגְלָם הַיְמָנִית וַיִּזְרֹק מֹשֶׁה אֶת־הַדָּם עַל־הַמִּזְבֵּחַ סָבִיב׃

Moses then brought forward the sons of Aaron, and put some of the blood on the ridges of their right ears, and on the thumbs of their right hands, and on the big toes of their right feet; and the rest of the blood Moses dashed against every side of the altar.

Author's Note: This parsha, which focuses on the inauguration of the mishkan along with Aharon and his sons as priests, is full of intricate staging, with Moshe as the dedicated director & producer. It ends on a note of anticipation—the process is almost done, the mishkan is almost ready. It's only at the beginning of Parshat Shemini that we get the grand finale—the final offering, the consuming fire, the adoring crowd.

Shemini

what if I want to seek out
your holiness; what if I want
more than you have given me;
if I want to see myself wrapped in
you, bound to you, bearing my heart's
strange fire on clean, unblemished palms.

> **Leviticus 10:1-2**
> וַיִּקְחוּ בְנֵי־אַהֲרֹן נָדָב וַאֲבִיהוּא אִישׁ מַחְתָּתוֹ וַיִּתְּנוּ
> בָהֵן אֵשׁ וַיָּשִׂימוּ עָלֶיהָ קְטֹרֶת וַיַּקְרִיבוּ לִפְנֵי יְהֹוָה
> אֵשׁ זָרָה אֲשֶׁר לֹא צִוָּה אֹתָם: וַתֵּצֵא אֵשׁ מִלִּפְנֵי
> יְהֹוָה וַתֹּאכַל אוֹתָם וַיָּמֻתוּ לִפְנֵי יְהֹוָה:
> Now Aaron's sons Nadab and Abihu each
> took his fire pan, put fire in it, and laid
> incense on it; and they offered beforeHashem
> alien fire, which had not been enjoined upon
> them. And fire came forth from Hashem and
> consumed them; thus they died before
> Hashem.

what if I tapped on each stone waiting to hear
your echo, and I was ready to be kissed with holy
flames—to leave nothing behind but this empty,
reaching form.

> **Leviticus 9:24**
> וַתֵּצֵא אֵשׁ מִלִּפְנֵי יְהֹוָה וַתֹּאכַל עַל־הַמִּזְבֵּחַ אֶת־הָעֹלָה וְאֶת־הַחֲלָבִים וַיַּרְא כָּל־הָעָם וַיָּרֹנּוּ
> וַיִּפְּלוּ עַל־פְּנֵיהֶם:
> Fire came forth from before Hashem and consumed the burnt offering and the fat
> parts on the altar. And all the people saw, and shouted, and fell on their faces.

> **Ibn Ezra on Leviticus 10:2**
> AND THEY DIED BEFORE THE LORD. They
> thought that they were doing something favorable before
> Them.

> **Nechama Leibowitz, Parshat Shemini**
> Evidently, Nadav and Avihu did not offend against any ritual precepts but
> sinned by reaching for God through the dictates of their own hearts rather
> than through the path set by God. Submission to the yoke of Heaven — the
> ultimate aim of the Torah — was here supplanted by unbridled religious
> ecstasy. Hence their punishment.

> **Yerushalmi Shekalim 6:1**
> But the rabbis say, the Ark was hidden in the storage room of the wood. It happened that a blemished
> Cohen was splitting wood in the storage room of the wood and saw a floor plate different from the others.
> He came and said to a colleague, come and see this floor plate which is different from the others. They did
> not finish the matter before his soul left him; then they knew that there the Ark was hidden. Rebbi
> Hoshaia stated: He hit on it with a sledgehammer; fire erupted and burned him.

Tazria–Metzora

it took God 80 days to
make me, I counted—
40 days to play in the
mud and blow it kisses,
40 days to shape bend fashion
a head mouth hair eyes
breasts and toes that, on
the 80th day, wiggled in the
mud with joy, and

see, when I clutch my
baby girl to my chest for
80 days, purified in water,
purified in blood, and her
body warm and small and
perfect and mine,
it's only *imitatio dei*,
I only wanted to keep her
a little longer, God,
make sure we've worked
out every kink and

watch, on the 80th day
I'll pry her fingers softly
from my shoulders, send
her into the world with a braid
in her hair and one kiss on
her wrinkled brow.

Leviticus 12:5

וְאִם־נְקֵבָה תֵלֵד וְטָמְאָה שְׁבֻעַיִם כְּנִדָּתָהּ וְשִׁשִּׁים יוֹם וְשֵׁשֶׁת יָמִים
תֵּשֵׁב עַל־דְּמֵי טָהֳרָה:

If she bears a female, she shall be impure two weeks as during
her menstruation, and she shall remain in a state of blood
purification for sixty-six days.

Niddah 30b

It can therefore be inferred that just as when the verse deems a
woman impure and then deems her pure for a total of forty days
in the case of a male, its amount of time is parallel to the time of
the formation of a male embryo; so too, when the verse deems a
woman impure and deems her pure for a total of eighty days in
the case of a female, its amount of time is parallel to the time of
the formation of a female embryo.

Jubilees 3:8-9

In the first week, Adam and the flank, his wife, were
fashioned, and in the second week They showed her to him.
And for this reason a commandment was given to maintain
[postpartum mothers] – seven days for a male [child] and
for a female two seven-day [units] – in their impurity.

Afterwards, when for Adam forty days had been completed
in the land where he had been fashioned, we brought him
into the Garden of Eden to till and maintain it. And his wife
was brought [there] on the eightieth day. Afterwards, she
entered into the Garden of Eden.

Shabbat 95a

Yes, braiding one's hair is considered building, as
Rabbi Shimon ben Menasya taught that the verse
states: "And the Lord God built the side that They
took from Adam into a woman" (Genesis 2:22),
which teaches that the Holy One, Blessed be They,
braided Eve's hair and brought her to Adam.

Acharei Mot-Kedoshim

oh we sit here in breathless
anxiety waiting for the
lot to fall, ears flicking
to and fro hoofs trodding
the dirt mindlessly and our
thoughts only,
which we will be
our thoughts only,
what can I want, and

can I see myself bound
and slaughtered, just
a singed scent of purity
and sin and a sprinkle of
blood on the tent walls and
oh, I would be so clean
and so dead

or, those hands set upon
me and a soft voice in my
ear, whispering truths until
the sin sits heavy in my
hair and a small rope around
my neck and I am off, I am
free in the wilderness of Azazel or
I am off, I am plunging down
the mountainside or I
am off, in the hands of
Azazel and I suppose

you won't need to look
back at my broken body,
either way you'll walk
away from me like the world's
been lifted off your shoulders
one hand pumping the sky with
my blood still caught on your
fingertips and you will be
so clean, so clean.

Leviticus 16:7-10

וְלָקַח אֶת־שְׁנֵי הַשְּׂעִירִם וְהֶעֱמִיד אֹתָם לִפְנֵי יְהֹוָה פֶּתַח אֹהֶל מוֹעֵד: וְנָתַן אַהֲרֹן עַל־שְׁנֵי הַשְּׂעִירִם גֹּרָלוֹת גּוֹרָל אֶחָד לַיהֹוָה וְגוֹרָל אֶחָד לַעֲזָאזֵל: וְהִקְרִיב אַהֲרֹן אֶת־הַשָּׂעִיר אֲשֶׁר עָלָה עָלָיו הַגּוֹרָל לַיהֹוָה וְעָשָׂהוּ חַטָּאת: וְהַשָּׂעִיר אֲשֶׁר עָלָה עָלָיו הַגּוֹרָל לַעֲזָאזֵל יׇעֳמַד־חַי לִפְנֵי יְהֹוָה לְכַפֵּר עָלָיו לְשַׁלַּח אֹתוֹ לַעֲזָאזֵל הַמִּדְבָּרָה:

Aaron shall take the two he-goats and let them stand before Hashem at the entrance of the Tent of Meeting; and he shall place lots upon the two goats, one marked for Hashem and the other marked for Azazel. Aaron shall bring forward the goat designated by lot for Hashem, which he is to offer as a sin offering; while the goat designated by lot for Azazel shall be left standing alive before Hashem, to make expiation with it and to send it off to the wilderness for Azazel.

Sifra, Acharei Mot, Chapter 2:6

Why is it stated that it shall be presented alive; this is already implied in the word יעמד. it shall be made to stand!? But because it continues "to send it forth unto Azazel" and I would not know whether this "sending forth" means to death or to life, therefore Scripture states "it shall be presented alive" — its presentation must be made whilst it is alive and the animal remains so up to the time when it is being sent forth; it follows therefore that it shall be sent forth to death.

Leviticus 16:21-22

וְסָמַךְ אַהֲרֹן אֶת־שְׁתֵּי יָדָו עַל רֹאשׁ הַשָּׂעִיר הַחַי וְהִתְוַדָּה עָלָיו אֶת־כׇּל־עֲוֺנֹת בְּנֵי יִשְׂרָאֵל וְאֶת־כׇּל־פִּשְׁעֵיהֶם לְכׇל־חַטֹּאתָם וְנָתַן אֹתָם עַל־רֹאשׁ הַשָּׂעִיר וְשִׁלַּח בְּיַד־אִישׁ עִתִּי הַמִּדְבָּרָה: וְנָשָׂא הַשָּׂעִיר עָלָיו אֶת־כׇּל־עֲוֺנֹתָם אֶל־אֶרֶץ גְּזֵרָה וְשִׁלַּח אֶת־הַשָּׂעִיר בַּמִּדְבָּר:

Aaron shall lay both his hands upon the head of the live goat and confess over it all the iniquities and transgressions of the Israelites, whatever their sins, putting them on the head of the goat; and it shall be sent off to the wilderness through a designated agent. Thus the goat shall carry on it all their iniquities to an inaccessible region; and the goat shall be set free in the wilderness.

Mishna Yoma 6:3-4,6

After the confession over the scapegoat, the priest passed the goat to the one who was to lead it to the wilderness...And they made a ramp for the goat due to the Babylonian Jews who were in Jerusalem, who would pluck at the goat's hair and would say to the goat: Take our sins and go, take our sins and go, and do not leave them with us...What did the one designated to dispatch the goat do there? He divided a strip of crimson into two parts, half of the strip tied to the rock, and half of it tied between the two horns of the goat. And he pushed the goat backward, and it rolls and descends. And it would not reach halfway down the mountain until it was torn limb from limb.

Emor

see, I can never quite reckon it—that you come closest to the broken-hearted, that there is nothing quite so whole as our fractured selves and this, maybe, is why we're your very favorites (and oh we won't tell)—the angels are too perfect to ever make of themselves a shattered offering, to you, and it is only through these cracks that you see our yearning and yet,

I must be somehow both broken and perfect and

see I only half-know, God, why my sacrifice of a broken heart must be held up to you on smooth, unblemished palms.

Ramban Leviticus 1:9
All these acts are performed in order that when they are done, a person should realize that he has sinned against his G-d with his body and his soul, and that "his" blood should really be spilled and "his" body burned, were it not for the loving-kindness of the Creator, Who took from him a substitute and a ransom, namely this offering, so that its blood should be in place of his blood, its life in place of his life, and that the chief limbs of the offering should be in place of the chief parts of his body.

Psalms 34:19
קָרוֹב יְהוָה לְנִשְׁבְּרֵי־לֵב וְאֶת־דַּכְּאֵי־רוּחַ יוֹשִׁיעַ:
Hashem is close to the broken-hearted; those crushed in spirit They deliver.

Psalms 51:19
זִבְחֵי אֱלֹהִים רוּחַ נִשְׁבָּרָה לֵב־נִשְׁבָּר וְנִדְכֶּה אֱלֹהִים לֹא תִבְזֶה:
True sacrifice to God is a broken spirit; God, do not scorn a crushed and despondent heart.

Rabbi Menachem Mendel of Kotzk
There is nothing so whole as a broken heart.

Avodat Yisrael, Sefer Devarim, Re'eh
However the matter is that the dwellers on high are certainly above the dwellers on low (humans), but the dwellers on low are more beloved. For the service of angels does not inspire delight, since they serve constantly and without choice. But the [service] of Yisrael who dwell below, who wage war against their evil inclination and conquer it, who turn from the bad and do what is good and upright... their service inspires delight.

Leviticus 21:21, 23
כָּל־אִישׁ אֲשֶׁר־בּוֹ מוּם מִזֶּרַע אַהֲרֹן הַכֹּהֵן לֹא יִגַּשׁ לְהַקְרִיב אֶת־אִשֵּׁי יְהוָה מוּם בּוֹ אֵת לֶחֶם אֱלֹהָיו לֹא יִגַּשׁ לְהַקְרִיב:
...אֶל־הַפָּרֹכֶת לֹא יָבֹא וְאֶל־הַמִּזְבֵּחַ לֹא יִגַּשׁ כִּי־מוּם בּוֹ וְלֹא יְחַלֵּל אֶת־מִקְדָּשַׁי כִּי אֲנִי יְהוָה מְקַדְּשָׁם:
No man among the offspring of Aaron the priest who has a defect shall be qualified to offer Hashem offering by fire; having a defect, he shall not be qualified to offer the food of his God... he shall not enter behind the curtain or come near the altar, for he has a defect. He shall not profane these places sacred to Me, for I Hashem have sanctified them.

Behar

we are all strange
we who dwell here
what is ours is not ours
and the land returns

come back
return to this place
after seven times seven
the land returns

take your food from God
let your fields grow wild
and you will be free
when the land returns.

> **Leviticus 25:23**
> וְהָאָ֗רֶץ לֹ֤א תִמָּכֵר֙ לִצְמִתֻ֔ת כִּי־לִ֖י
> הָאָ֑רֶץ כִּֽי־גֵרִ֧ים וְתוֹשָׁבִ֛ים אַתֶּ֖ם
> עִמָּדִֽי:
> But the land must not be sold
> beyond reclaim, for the land
> is Mine; you are but
> strangers dwelling with Me

Behar-Bechukotai

Exodus 19:6
וְאַתֶּם תִּהְיוּ־לִי מַמְלֶכֶת כֹּהֲנִים וְגוֹי קָדוֹשׁ...
But you shall be to Me a kingdom of priests and a holy nation.

Leviticus 26:3-5
אִם־בְּחֻקֹּתַי תֵּלֵכוּ וְאֶת־מִצְוֹתַי תִּשְׁמְרוּ וַעֲשִׂיתֶם אֹתָם: וְנָתַתִּי גִשְׁמֵיכֶם בְּעִתָּם וְנָתְנָה הָאָרֶץ יְבוּלָהּ וְעֵץ הַשָּׂדֶה יִתֵּן פִּרְיוֹ: וְהִשִּׂיג לָכֶם דַּיִשׁ אֶת־בָּצִיר וּבָצִיר יַשִּׂיג אֶת־זָרַע וַאֲכַלְתֶּם לַחְמְכֶם לָשֹׂבַע וִישַׁבְתֶּם לָבֶטַח בְּאַרְצְכֶם:
If you follow My laws and faithfully observe My commandments, I will grant your rains in their season, so that the earth shall yield its produce and the trees of the field their fruit. Your threshing shall overtake the vintage, and your vintage shall overtake the sowing; you shall eat your fill of bread and dwell securely in your land.

Leviticus 26:11
וְנָתַתִּי מִשְׁכָּנִי בְּתוֹכְכֶם וְלֹא־תִגְעַל נַפְשִׁי אֶתְכֶם:
I will establish My abode in your midst, and I will not loathe you.

Rashi on Leviticus 25:35
THOU SHALT RELIEVE HIM (*vehechezakta bo*)
Do not leave [your struggling kin] by himself so that he comes down in the world until he finally falls altogether when it will be difficult to give him a lift, but uphold him from the very moment of the failure of his means. To what may this be compared? To an excessive load on the back of an ass. So long as it is still on the ass's back, one person is enough to take hold of it (the load) and to keep it (the ass) up, as soon as it has fallen to the ground not even five persons are able to set it on its legs (Sifra, Behar, Section 5:1).

Leviticus 26:6
וְנָתַתִּי שָׁלוֹם בָּאָרֶץ וּשְׁכַבְתֶּם וְאֵין מַחֲרִיד וְהִשְׁבַּתִּי חַיָּה רָעָה מִן־הָאָרֶץ וְחֶרֶב לֹא־תַעֲבֹר בְּאַרְצְכֶם:
I will grant peace in the land, and you shall lie down untroubled by anyone; I will give the land respite from vicious beasts, and no sword shall cross your land.

if only you follow these laws,
my *am segulah*,
my kingdom of priests
my holy nation,
I will dwell amongst you—
the land will sing growth
and the food will sit full
in your soft & swelling stomachs,
will I love you?
I will not loathe you.

vehechezakta bo,
it is so much easier to
prevent disaster than to
reverse it.

until you rid this land of vicious beasts,
I cannot promise that you
may lie down.

this land is yours when you are holy,
holy nation.

hashiva shofteinu k'varishonah,
there is no perfect past to which
I can restore you, just this,
the sacred future you shape.

11th Prayer in the Weekday Amidah
Restore our judges (*hashiva shofteinu*) as in days of old and our counselors as at first. Remove sorrow and sighing from us, and reign over us You, Adonoy, alone with kindness and compassion; and make us righteous with justice.

Bamidbar

Kli Yakar on Bamidbar 1:1
Rashi explains that on the day the Mishkon was erected, the Israelites were like a bride entering the wedding canopy. This teaches us that the Giving of the Torah was like betrothal (erusin), and the day the Mishkon was erected was like marriage (nisuin).

Yoma 54a
Rav Nachman said in answer: This is analogous to a bride; as long as she is engaged but still in her father's house, she is modest in the presence of her husband. However, once she is married and comes to her father-in-law's house to live with her husband, she is no longer modest in the presence of her husband.

strip off your wedding garments, my groom— I'll carry you on my bare shoulders and cradle you so gently and together we will be lost, ownerless, wandering, untethered, bound.

Numbers 4:15
וְכִלָּה אַהֲרֹן־וּבָנָיו לְכַסֹּת אֶת־הַקֹּדֶשׁ וְאֶת־כָּל־כְּלֵי הַקֹּדֶשׁ בִּנְסֹעַ הַמַּחֲנֶה וְאַחֲרֵי־כֵן יָבֹאוּ בְנֵי־קְהָת לָשֵׂאת וְלֹא־יִגְּעוּ אֶל־הַקֹּדֶשׁ וָמֵתוּ.
When Aaron and his sons have finished covering the sacred objects and all the furnishings of the sacred objects at the breaking of camp, only then shall the Kohathites come and lift them, so that they do not come in contact with the sacred objects and die.

Avigayil Halpern, "Bamidbar: Vulnerability"
The holy vessels of the Mishkan are compared to a bride. When she is engaged, before her wedding, she remains dressed in front of her husband, but after she is married and goes to live with him, she can undress. So too, the sacred vessels must be dressed in front of the Jewish people — to whom, in this analogy, they are married, or perhaps they represent God, to whom the Jewish people are married — while they are in the desert. Once they are "home" in the Temple, they can be — literally! — undressed.

Naso

you can pour the
bitter waters down
my throat, all at once,

you can hear me say
amen amen amen amen
and I'll swallow every
word, gulp them down

with a smile, and you'll
stare, maybe wondering
why it is these words of

Torah can't catch in my
throat but slide down
sweetly, smooth as milk,
smooth as honey.

**Alicia Jo Rabins, "Secrets/You're Always
Watching" from *Girls in Trouble***
He took me downtown and he gave me the jar of water
The people watched as I brought it to my lips
He said if you're guilty your body will betray you
But I know how to be silent after a kiss

Numbers 5:16-24

וְהִקְרִיב אֹתָהּ הַכֹּהֵן וְהֶעֱמִדָהּ לִפְנֵי יְהֹוָה: וְלָקַח הַכֹּהֵן מַיִם
קְדֹשִׁים בִּכְלִי־חָרֶשׂ וּמִן־הֶעָפָר אֲשֶׁר יִהְיֶה בְּקַרְקַע הַמִּשְׁכָּן
יִקַּח הַכֹּהֵן וְנָתַן אֶל־הַמָּיִם: וְהֶעֱמִיד הַכֹּהֵן אֶת־הָאִשָּׁה לִפְנֵי
יְהֹוָה וּפָרַע אֶת־רֹאשׁ הָאִשָּׁה וְנָתַן עַל־כַּפֶּיהָ אֵת מִנְחַת
הַזִּכָּרוֹן מִנְחַת קְנָאֹת הִוא וּבְיַד הַכֹּהֵן יִהְיוּ מֵי הַמָּרִים
הַמְאָרֲרִים: וְהִשְׁבִּיעַ אֹתָהּ הַכֹּהֵן וְאָמַר אֶל־הָאִשָּׁה אִם־לֹא
שָׁכַב אִישׁ אֹתָךְ וְאִם־לֹא שָׂטִית טֻמְאָה תַּחַת אִישֵׁךְ הִנָּקִי מִמֵּי
הַמָּרִים הַמְאָרֲרִים הָאֵלֶּה: וְאַתְּ כִּי שָׂטִית תַּחַת אִישֵׁךְ וְכִי
נִטְמֵאת וַיִּתֵּן אִישׁ בָּךְ אֶת־שְׁכָבְתּוֹ מִבַּלְעֲדֵי אִישֵׁךְ: וְהִשְׁבִּיעַ
הַכֹּהֵן אֶת־הָאִשָּׁה בִּשְׁבֻעַת הָאָלָה וְאָמַר הַכֹּהֵן לָאִשָּׁה יִתֵּן
יְהֹוָה אוֹתָךְ לְאָלָה וְלִשְׁבֻעָה בְּתוֹךְ עַמֵּךְ בְּתֵת יְהֹוָה אֶת־יְרֵכֵךְ
נֹפֶלֶת וְאֶת־בִּטְנֵךְ צָבָה: וּבָאוּ הַמַּיִם הַמְאָרֲרִים הָאֵלֶּה בְּמֵעַיִךְ
לַצְבּוֹת בֶּטֶן וְלַנְפִּל יָרֵךְ וְאָמְרָה הָאִשָּׁה אָמֵן | אָמֵן: וְכָתַב
אֶת־הָאָלֹת הָאֵלֶּה הַכֹּהֵן בַּסֵּפֶר וּמָחָה אֶל־מֵי הַמָּרִים:
וְהִשְׁקָה אֶת־הָאִשָּׁה אֶת־מֵי הַמָּרִים הַמְאָרֲרִים וּבָאוּ בָהּ
הַמַּיִם הַמְאָרֲרִים לְמָרִים:

The priest shall bring forward [the woman suspected of
adultery] and have her stand before Hashem. The priest
shall take sacral water in an earthen vessel and, taking
some of the earth that is on the floor of the Tabernacle,
the priest shall put it into the water. After he has made the
woman stand before Hashem, the priest shall bare the
woman's head... And in the priest's hands shall be the
water of bitterness that induces the spell. The priest shall
adjure the woman, saying to her, "If no other party has
lain with you, if you have not gone astray in defilement
while living in your husband's household, be immune to
harm from this water of bitterness that induces the spell.
But if you have gone astray while living in your husband's
household and have defiled yourself, if any party other
than your husband has had carnal relations with you...
may Hashem make you a curse and an imprecation among
your people, as Hashem causes your thigh to sag and your
belly to distend; may this water that induces the spell
enter your body, causing the belly to distend and the
thigh to sag." And the woman shall say, "Amen, amen!"
The priest shall put these curses down in writing and rub
it off into the water of bitterness. He is to make the
woman drink the water of bitterness that induces the
spell, so that the spell-inducing water may enter into her
to bring on bitterness.

Author's Note: I think a lot about the sotah ritual being the only instance in which
we're allowed to erase passages of Torah—the very passage quoted here. I think
a lot about the woman swallowing Hashem's name. I think about her
experience of hurt and vindication.

Beha'alotkha

and see what if,
what if we were
all prophets, can
you imagine for
a moment,

god's words on
everyone's lips
and

no room for the
false prophet
industry, no
fake salvation,
no half-way
justice,

would that every
one of us were
prophets, you
catch us wandering
through the streets
speaking tongues,
or

is it speaking
tongues if we
all form the same
words, if we all
share one voice
and,

can you imagine
how it would
feel, to be
a prophet and
to be heard?
and

can you see
how if we were
all, all of us,
prophets,

this burden
wouldn't be
too heavy to
bear.

Numbers 11:14
לֹא־אוּכַל אָנֹכִי לְבַדִּי לָשֵׂאת
אֶת־כָּל־הָעָם הַזֶּה כִּי כָבֵד
מִמֶּנִּי:
I cannot carry all this
people by myself, for it is
too much for me.

Numbers 11:16-17
וַיֹּאמֶר יְהֹוָה אֶל־מֹשֶׁה
אֶסְפָה־לִּי שִׁבְעִים אִישׁ מִזִּקְנֵי
יִשְׂרָאֵל אֲשֶׁר יָדַעְתָּ כִּי־הֵם
זִקְנֵי הָעָם וְשֹׁטְרָיו וְלָקַחְתָּ
אֹתָם אֶל־אֹהֶל מוֹעֵד וְהִתְיַצְּבוּ
שָׁם עִמָּךְ: וְיָרַדְתִּי וְדִבַּרְתִּי
עִמְּךָ שָׁם וְאָצַלְתִּי מִן־הָרוּחַ
אֲשֶׁר עָלֶיךָ וְשַׂמְתִּי עֲלֵיהֶם
וְנָשְׂאוּ אִתְּךָ בְּמַשָּׂא הָעָם
וְלֹא־תִשָּׂא אַתָּה לְבַדֶּךָ:
Then Hashem said to
Moses, "Gather for Me
seventy of Israel's elders of
whom you have experience
as elders and officers of the
people, and bring them to
the Tent of Meeting and let
them take their place there
with you. I will come down
and speak with you there,
and I will draw upon the
spirit that is on you and put
it upon them; they shall
share the burden of the
people with you, and you
shall not bear it alone."

Numbers 11:26, 28-29

וַיִּשָּׁאֲר֣וּ שְׁנֵֽי־אֲנָשִׁ֣ים | בַּֽמַּחֲנֶ֡ה שֵׁ֣ם
הָאֶחָ֣ד | אֶלְדָּ֡ד וְשֵׁם֩ הַשֵּׁנִ֨י מֵידָ֜ד
וַתָּ֧נַח עֲלֵהֶ֣ם הָר֗וּחַ וְהֵ֙מָּה֙ בַּכְּתֻבִ֔ים
וְלֹ֥א יָצְא֖וּ הָאֹ֑הֱלָה וַיִּֽתְנַבְּא֖וּ
בַּֽמַּחֲנֶֽה: ...וַיַּ֜עַן יְהוֹשֻׁ֣עַ בִּן־נ֗וּן
מְשָׁרֵ֥ת מֹשֶׁ֛ה מִבְּחֻרָ֖יו וַיֹּאמַ֑ר אֲדֹנִ֥י
מֹשֶׁ֖ה כְּלָאֵֽם: וַיֹּ֤אמֶר לוֹ֙ מֹשֶׁ֔ה
הַֽמְקַנֵּ֥א אַתָּ֖ה לִ֑י וּמִ֨י יִתֵּ֜ן כָּל־עַ֤ם
יְהוָה֙ נְבִיאִ֔ים כִּֽי־יִתֵּ֧ן יְהוָ֛ה אֶת־רוּח֖וֹ
עֲלֵיהֶֽם:

Two of the participants, one
named Eldad and the other
Medad, had remained in camp;
yet the spirit rested upon them
—they were among those
recorded, but they had not gone
out to the Tent—and they
prophesied in the camp...
And Joshua son of Nun, Moses'
attendant from his youth, spoke
up and said, "My lord Moses,
restrain them!" But Moses said
to him, "Are you jealous on my
account? Would that all
Hashem's people were prophets,
that Hashem put [the divine]
spirit upon them!"

68

if I am truly their mother,
if I have born and suckled
them, what more have I to
give than this—these daily
offerings of sweet, rich cream,
as soft and constant as the
dew. how much longer can I
hear these earsplitting wails and
know there's no more I can offer—
that when their teeth clamp down,
gnawing and desperate, they'll meet
nothing but a steady flow of milk.

Author's Note: As you'll see in the coming parsha and much of Devarim, I'm deeply interested in Moshe's relationship with B'nei Yisrael, the pain and frustration and intimacy of it, and the ways in which Moshe embodies the role of parent—often, the aggrieved mother coparenting with Hashem, an authoritative and more distant father. His complaint here is typically cast as a rejection of that role—an insistence that he is not B'nei Yisrael's mother, to nurse and to carry them. But I chose to imagine it in a different light; one in which Moshe accepts the role of mother, and is hurt and distressed that for B'nei Yisrael this is still not enough. He can nurse them with manna and torah, which are compared to breast milk, but they wish to be weaned.

Sh'lach

when I came down the mountain after 40 days
with honey on my tongue and milk in my breasts
I said *it is sweet* and I said *it is nourishing* and
you did not believe me;
but when they come down from the land after 40 days
laden with grapes pomegranate juice sticky on their lips
and they say *it is too rich* they say *it is bitter* they say
you will not devour, you will be devoured,
you fall to hopeless weeping. you do not even ask for
a taste.

Numbers 13:23

וַיָּבֹאוּ עַד־נַחַל אֶשְׁכֹּל
וַיִּכְרְתוּ מִשָּׁם זְמוֹרָה
וְאֶשְׁכּוֹל עֲנָבִים אֶחָד
וַיִּשָּׂאֻהוּ בַמּוֹט בִּשְׁנָיִם
וּמִן־הָרִמֹּנִים
וּמִן־הַתְּאֵנִים:

[The spies] reached
the wadi Eshcol, and
there they cut down a
branch with a single
cluster of grapes—it
had to be borne on a
carrying frame by two
of them—and some
pomegranates and figs.

Exodus 24:18

וַיָּבֹא מֹשֶׁה בְּתוֹךְ הֶעָנָן וַיַּעַל אֶל־הָהָר וַיְהִי
מֹשֶׁה בָּהָר אַרְבָּעִים יוֹם וְאַרְבָּעִים לָיְלָה:

Moses went inside the cloud and
ascended the mountain; and Moses
remained on the mountain forty days and
forty nights.

Numbers 13:25, 27-28, 31-32

וַיָּשֻׁבוּ מִתּוּר הָאָרֶץ מִקֵּץ אַרְבָּעִים יוֹם: ...וַיְסַפְּרוּ־לוֹ וַיֹּאמְרוּ בָּאנוּ
אֶל־הָאָרֶץ אֲשֶׁר שְׁלַחְתָּנוּ וְגַם זָבַת חָלָב וּדְבַשׁ הִוא וְזֶה־פִּרְיָהּ:
אֶפֶס כִּי־עַז הָעָם הַיֹּשֵׁב בָּאָרֶץ וְהֶעָרִים בְּצֻרוֹת גְּדֹלֹת מְאֹד
וְגַם־יְלִדֵי הָעֲנָק רָאִינוּ שָׁם: ...וְהָאֲנָשִׁים אֲשֶׁר־עָלוּ עִמּוֹ אָמְרוּ לֹא
נוּכַל לַעֲלוֹת אֶל־הָעָם כִּי־חָזָק הוּא מִמֶּנּוּ: וַיֹּצִיאוּ דִּבַּת הָאָרֶץ
אֲשֶׁר תָּרוּ אֹתָהּ אֶל־בְּנֵי יִשְׂרָאֵל לֵאמֹר הָאָרֶץ אֲשֶׁר עָבַרְנוּ בָהּ
לָתוּר אֹתָהּ אֶרֶץ אֹכֶלֶת יוֹשְׁבֶיהָ הִוא...

At the end of forty days they returned from scouting the
land...This is what they told [Moshe]: "We came to the land
you sent us to; it does indeed flow with milk and honey, and
this is its fruit. However, the people who inhabit the country
are powerful, and the cities are fortified and very large...We
cannot attack that people, for it is stronger than we. Thus
they spread calumnies among the Israelites about the land
they had scouted, saying, "The country that we traversed
and scouted is one that devours its inhabitants..."

Shir HaShirim Rabbah 4:5:1

"Your breasts are like two fawns."
Just as these breasts are the
splendor and glory of a woman, so
too Moses and Aaron are the
splendor and glory of Israel... Just
like these breasts are full of milk,
Moses and Aaron fill Israel with
Torah. And just as with these
breasts, all that a woman eats, the
baby eats and nurses from them,
so too all of the Torah that Moses
learned he taught to Aaron.

Numbers 14:1

וַתִּשָּׂא כָּל־הָעֵדָה וַיִּתְּנוּ אֶת־קוֹלָם וַיִּבְכּוּ הָעָם בַּלַּיְלָה הַהוּא:
The whole community broke into loud cries, and the people
wept that night.

if only you'd
sewn fringes on
our garments
the moment we
set foot outside
Egypt, if we could
have watched them
swing wildly around
us as the sea came
crashing down and we'd
seen threads of sky-
blue, heaven blue
wheel around our hips
as they kept to the
timbrels' tempo, perhaps
we would not have
complained so fiercely or
so frequently; perhaps
we would have felt
ourselves girded in
slim strings, surrounded
by mitzvot (that the kids
tug on, swiftly, for
attention), and known
we were never really
free.

Numbers 15:38-40

דַּבֵּר אֶל־בְּנֵי יִשְׂרָאֵל וְאָמַרְתָּ אֲלֵהֶם וְעָשׂוּ לָהֶם צִיצִת עַל־כַּנְפֵי בִגְדֵיהֶם לְדֹרֹתָם וְנָתְנוּ עַל־צִיצִת הַכָּנָף פְּתִיל תְּכֵלֶת: וְהָיָה לָכֶם לְצִיצִת וּרְאִיתֶם אֹתוֹ וּזְכַרְתֶּם אֶת־כָּל־מִצְוֹת יְהוָה וַעֲשִׂיתֶם אֹתָם וְלֹא־תָתוּרוּ אַחֲרֵי לְבַבְכֶם וְאַחֲרֵי עֵינֵיכֶם אֲשֶׁר־אַתֶּם זֹנִים אַחֲרֵיהֶם: לְמַעַן תִּזְכְּרוּ וַעֲשִׂיתֶם אֶת־כָּל־מִצְוֹתָי וִהְיִיתֶם קְדֹשִׁים לֵאלֹהֵיכֶם:

Speak to the Israelite people and instruct them to make for themselves fringes on the corners of their garments throughout the ages; let them attach a cord of blue to the fringe at each corner. That shall be your fringe; look at it and recall all the commandments of יהוה and observe them, so that you do not follow your heart and eyes in your lustful urge. Thus you shall be reminded to observe all My commandments and to be holy to your God.

Shavuot 29a

The Master says: The mitzva of ritual fringes is equivalent to all the other mitzvot.

Menachot 43b

It is taught in a baraita that Rabbi Meir would say: What is different about tekhelet from all other types of colors such that it was chosen for the mitzva of ritual fringes? It is because tekhelet is similar in its color to the sea, and the sea is similar to the sky, and the sky is similar to the Throne of Glory...

HaAmek Davar on Leviticus 25:55

FOR IT IS TO ME [God] THAT THE ISRAELITES ARE SLAVES. They became enslaved to me with the acceptance of the Torah.

Korach

we are not all holy, but we can be, she murmurs, dribbling wine between his stubborn lips and laying him down softly on the earth. she sits at the entrance of the tent her bare hair a curtain flap her bare hair brushing his cheeks so gently that he cannot look away, and they cannot look toward him. not all promises are worth keeping, she insists, lifting a furious gaze to any who dare pass by. we all can be holy, she says, drawing her hair into thick braids. in between her darting fingers, he sees the earth begin to open its mouth wide.

Numbers 16:1-3

וַיִּקַּח קֹרַח בֶּן־יִצְהָר בֶּן־קְהָת בֶּן־לֵוִי וְדָתָן וַאֲבִירָם בְּנֵי אֱלִיאָב וְאוֹן בֶּן־פֶּלֶת בְּנֵי רְאוּבֵן: וַיָּקֻמוּ לִפְנֵי מֹשֶׁה וַאֲנָשִׁים מִבְּנֵי־יִשְׂרָאֵל חֲמִשִּׁים וּמָאתָיִם נְשִׂיאֵי עֵדָה קְרִאֵי מוֹעֵד אַנְשֵׁי־שֵׁם: וַיִּקָּהֲלוּ עַל־מֹשֶׁה וְעַל־אַהֲרֹן וַיֹּאמְרוּ אֲלֵהֶם רַב־לָכֶם כִּי כָל־הָעֵדָה כֻּלָּם קְדֹשִׁים וּבְתוֹכָם יְהוָה וּמַדּוּעַ תִּתְנַשְּׂאוּ עַל־קְהַל יְהוָה:

Now Korah, son of Izhar son of Kohath son of Levi, betook himself along with Dathan and Abiram sons of Eliab, and On son of Peleth—descendants of Reuben —to rise up against Moses, together with two hundred and fifty Israelites, chieftains of the community, chosen in the assembly, men of repute. They combined against Moses and Aaron and said to them, "You have gone too far! For all the community are holy, all of them, and Hashem is in their midst. Why then do you raise yourselves above Hashem's congregation?"

Numbers 16:24, 26, 31-33

דַּבֵּר אֶל־הָעֵדָה לֵאמֹר הֵעָלוּ מִסָּבִיב לְמִשְׁכַּן־קֹרַח דָּתָן וַאֲבִירָם: ...וַיְדַבֵּר אֶל־הָעֵדָה לֵאמֹר סוּרוּ נָא מֵעַל אָהֳלֵי הָאֲנָשִׁים הָרְשָׁעִים הָאֵלֶּה וְאַל־תִּגְּעוּ בְּכָל־אֲשֶׁר לָהֶם פֶּן־תִּסָּפוּ בְּכָל־חַטֹּאתָם: ...וַיְהִי כְּכַלֹּתוֹ לְדַבֵּר אֵת כָּל־הַדְּבָרִים הָאֵלֶּה וַתִּבָּקַע הָאֲדָמָה אֲשֶׁר תַּחְתֵּיהֶם: וַתִּפְתַּח הָאָרֶץ אֶת־פִּיהָ וַתִּבְלַע אֹתָם וְאֶת־בָּתֵּיהֶם וְאֵת כָּל־הָאָדָם אֲשֶׁר לְקֹרַח וְאֵת כָּל־הָרְכוּשׁ:

"Speak to the community and say: Withdraw from about the abodes of Korah, Dathan, and Abiram." ...[Moshe] addressed the community, saying, "Move away from the tents of these wicked men and touch nothing that belongs to them, lest you be wiped out for all their sins." ...Scarcely had he finished speaking all these words when the ground under them burst asunder, and the earth opened its mouth and swallowed them up with their households, all Korah's people and all their possessions.

Sanhedrin 109b-110a

Rav said: On ben Pelet: His wife saved him. She said to him: What will you get out of it [the rebellion against Moshe]? If the master [Moshe] is the leader, you are a student. And if the master [Korach] is the leader, you are a student. He said to her: What shall I do? I was in the [original] counsel and I swore together with them. She said to him: I know that the entire assembly is holy, as it is written: "For all the assembly is holy" (Numbers 16:3). She said to him: Sit down and I will save you. She gave him wine to drink and got him drunk and laid him inside [their tent]. She sat herself at the opening and let her hair loose. Whoever came [to call him] and saw her turned back. In the meantime, [the assembly of Korah] was swallowed [into the ground].

73

I have been told
that I am allowed only
some forms of rebellion,
that some are holy and
sweet and some will have
the earth swallow me
whole,

I have been told
rebellion is a gift
and a sin, that ours
is a religion of sacred
dispute and some things
must remain indisputable
and

I have seen that we are
a rebellion or a revolution
depending on which light
you cast,

I have seen that we
wish only to sanctify or
vilify rebellion retroactively,

that perhaps we thought
our lesson from Korach
is only that we are incapable
of discerning the holy fights
from the profane,

and now this is a people
all holy and all afraid and

I thought you should
know, we are still
called to challenge.
you are standing,
all of you,
on solid ground.

Eruvin 13b

Rabbi Abba said that Shmuel said: For three years Beit Shammai and Beit Hillel disagreed. These said: The halakha is in accordance with our opinion, and these said: The halakha is in accordance with our opinion. Ultimately, a Divine Voice emerged and proclaimed: Both these and those are the words of the living God.

Pirkei Avot 5:17

Every dispute that is for the sake of Heaven, will in the end endure; But one that is not for the sake of Heaven, will not endure. Which is the controversy that is for the sake of Heaven? Such was the controversy of Hillel and Shammai. And which is the controversy that is not for the sake of Heaven? Such was the controversy of Korah and all his congregation.

Chukat

We were without water
after her death
I remembered the rock
years ago
how I drew water from stone
sister beside me.
I struck the rock
again, without words
but time is like water
and drops into dust.
I, too, will die
in the desert.

Taanit 9a
Rabbi Yosei, son of
Rabbi Yehuda, says:
Three good sustainers
arose for the Jewish
people: Moses, Aaron
and Miriam. And three
good gifts were given
from Heaven through
their hands, and these
are they: the well, the
cloud, and the manna.
The well—in the merit
of Miriam; the cloud—
in the merit of Aaron;
and the manna—in the
merit of Moses. When
Miriam died the well
disappeared, as it is
stated: "And Miriam
died there" (Numbers
20:1), and it says
afterwards: "And there
was no water for the
congregation"
(Numbers 20:2).

Numbers 20:11-12

וַיָּ֨רֶם מֹשֶׁ֜ה אֶת־יָד֗וֹ וַיַּ֤ךְ אֶת־הַסֶּ֙לַע֙ בְּמַטֵּ֣הוּ פַּעֲמָ֔יִם וַיֵּצְאוּ֙ מַ֣יִם רַבִּ֔ים וַתֵּ֥שְׁתְּ הָעֵדָ֖ה וּבְעִירָֽם: וַיֹּ֣אמֶר יְהֹוָה֮ אֶל־מֹשֶׁ֣ה וְאֶֽל־אַהֲרֹן֒ יַ֚עַן
לֹא־הֶאֱמַנְתֶּ֣ם בִּ֔י לְהַ֨קְדִּישֵׁ֔נִי לְעֵינֵ֖י בְּנֵ֣י יִשְׂרָאֵ֑ל לָכֵ֗ן לֹ֤א תָבִ֙יאוּ֙ אֶת־הַקָּהָ֣ל הַזֶּ֔ה אֶל־הָאָ֖רֶץ אֲשֶׁר־נָתַ֥תִּי לָהֶֽם:

And Moses raised his hand and struck the rock twice with his rod. Out came copious water, and the community
and their beasts drank. But God said to Moses and Aaron, "Because you did not trust Me enough to affirm My
sanctity in the sight of the Israelite people, therefore you shall not lead this congregation into the land that I
have given them."

this time with no Miriam to lead us, we shake out our timbrels and dance with abandon, cries bursting from each rough, wet throat. we sing as our mothers did, the waters lapping at our feet, hopping about each severed limb. we sing that we are saved, we sing that we are sated.

Numbers 20:1

וַיָּבֹאוּ בְנֵי־יִשְׂרָאֵל כָּל־הָעֵדָה מִדְבַּר־צִן בַּחֹדֶשׁ הָרִאשׁוֹן וַיֵּשֶׁב הָעָם בְּקָדֵשׁ וַתָּמָת שָׁם מִרְיָם וַתִּקָּבֵר שָׁם: וְלֹא־הָיָה מַיִם לָעֵדָה וַיִּקָּהֲלוּ עַל־מֹשֶׁה וְעַל־אַהֲרֹן:

The Israelites arrived in a body at the wilderness of Zin on the first new moon, and the people stayed at Kadesh. Miriam died there and was buried there. The community was without water, and they joined against Moses and Aaron.

Numbers 20:11

וַיָּרֶם מֹשֶׁה אֶת־יָדוֹ וַיַּךְ אֶת־הַסֶּלַע בְּמַטֵּהוּ פַּעֲמָיִם וַיֵּצְאוּ מַיִם רַבִּים וַתֵּשְׁתְּ הָעֵדָה וּבְעִירָם:

And Moses raised his hand and struck the rock twice with his rod. Out came copious water, and the community and their beasts drank.

Numbers 21:3

וַיִּשְׁמַע יְהֹוָה בְּקוֹל יִשְׂרָאֵל וַיִּתֵּן אֶת־הַכְּנַעֲנִי וַיַּחֲרֵם אֶתְהֶם וְאֶת־עָרֵיהֶם וַיִּקְרָא שֵׁם־הַמָּקוֹם חָרְמָה:

Hashem heeded Israel's plea and delivered up the Canaanites; and they and their cities were proscribed. So that place was named Hormah.

Numbers 21:16-18

וּמִשָּׁם בְּאֵרָה הִוא הַבְּאֵר אֲשֶׁר אָמַר יְהֹוָה לְמֹשֶׁה אֱסֹף אֶת־הָעָם וְאֶתְּנָה לָהֶם מָיִם: אָז יָשִׁיר יִשְׂרָאֵל אֶת־הַשִּׁירָה הַזֹּאת עֲלִי בְאֵר עֱנוּ־לָהּ: בְּאֵר חֲפָרוּהָ שָׂרִים כָּרוּהָ נְדִיבֵי הָעָם בִּמְחֹקֵק בְּמִשְׁעֲנֹתָם וּמִמִּדְבָּר מַתָּנָה:

And [they went] from there to Beer which is the well where Hashem said to Moses, "Assemble the people that I may give them water." Then Israel sang this song: Spring up, O well—sing to it— The well which the chieftains dug, Which the nobles of the people started With maces, with their own staffs...

ᶜʰ

Midrash Tanchuma, Chukat 20

The crags entered into the caves and all those warriors were crushed. Then the well descended to the wadi, where it became a mighty [torrent] and destroyed the troops, just as the [Reed] Sea had destroyed those [Egyptians]... When Israel crossed upon those mountains without knowing about all these miracles the Holy One, blessed be They, said, "Behold, I will let My Children know how many troops I destroyed because of them." [So] the well descended into the caves and brought out innumerable skulls, arms, and legs. Thus when Israel returned to seek the well, they saw it shining like the moon in the midst of the wadi, as it discharged the limbs of the troops.

Mekhilta d'Rabbi Yishmael 14:31

"And Israel saw Egypt dead on the shore of the sea" (Exodus 14:30): The sea threw their bodies out on the shore so that the Israelites not say: Just as we came up on this side, so they came up on another side (and will pursue us).

Exodus 15:20

וַתִּקַּח֩ מִרְיָ֨ם הַנְּבִיאָ֜ה אֲח֧וֹת אַהֲרֹ֛ן אֶת־הַתֹּ֖ף בְּיָדָ֑הּ וַתֵּצֶ֤אןָ כׇל־הַנָּשִׁים֙ אַחֲרֶ֔יהָ בְּתֻפִּ֖ים וּבִמְחֹלֹֽת׃

Then Miriam the prophet, Aaron's sister, picked up a timbrel and all the women went out after her in dance with timbrels.

I'd like you to
know that Miriam
also died with a
kiss, that she was
gathered in so
softly, cool drops
of water still on the
tip of her tongue,
and she had not
expected it—
had felt she was
doomed only to
see G-d as a back
turned upon her,
and the kiss was
a sweet surprise,
a soft hello, a
welcoming back—
she was gathered
in with a quick *oh*
of the unexpected,
clear pools of water
still cupped in her
palms.

Rashi on Numbers 20:1
AND MIRIAM DIED THERE — She, too, as Moses and Aaron, died by a Divine Kiss (even though unlike with them, it is not said here explicitly).

Rashi on Numbers 20:2
AND THERE WAS NO WATER FOR THE CONGREGATION — Since this statement follows immediately after the mention of Miriam's death, we may learn from it that during the entire forty years they had the "well" through Miriam's merit (Taanit 9a).

Numbers 12:10
וְהֶעָנָן סָר מֵעַל הָאֹהֶל וְהִנֵּה מִרְיָם מְצֹרַעַת כַּשָּׁלֶג וַיִּפֶן אַהֲרֹן אֶל־מִרְיָם וְהִנֵּה מְצֹרָעַת:
As the cloud withdrew from the Tent, there was Miriam stricken with snow-white scales! When Aaron turned toward Miriam, he saw that she was stricken with scales.

Numbers 12:13-14
וַיִּצְעַק מֹשֶׁה אֶל־יְהוָה לֵאמֹר אֵל נָא רְפָא נָא לָהּ:
וַיֹּאמֶר יְהוָה אֶל־מֹשֶׁה וְאָבִיהָ יָרֹק יָרַק בְּפָנֶיהָ הֲלֹא תִכָּלֵם שִׁבְעַת יָמִים תִּסָּגֵר שִׁבְעַת יָמִים מִחוּץ לַמַּחֲנֶה וְאַחַר תֵּאָסֵף:
So Moses cried out to Hashem, saying, "O God, pray heal her!" But Hashem said to Moses, "If her father spat in her face, would she not bear her shame for seven days? Let her be shut out of camp for seven days, and then let her be readmitted."

Balak

like the lioness, enemy nations
dangling from her jaws, she and
her young greeting holy dawn with
a roar, fierce and touchy and lonely

like the lion, so proud in his lazy
kingship; so brilliant from afar, but
up close you see his yellowed teeth,
his tangled mine, and that great,
drooping head—crowned with glory,
heavy in defeat.

Numbers 23:24

הֶן־עָם֙ כְּלָבִ֣יא יָק֔וּם וְכַאֲרִ֖י יִתְנַשָּׂ֑א לֹ֤א יִשְׁכַּב֙ עַד־יֹ֣אכַל טֶ֔רֶף
וְדַם־חֲלָלִ֖ים יִשְׁתֶּֽה׃

Lo, a people that rises like a lioness,
Leaps up like a lion,
Rests not til it has feasted on prey
And drunk the blood of the slain.

Numbers 24:9

כָּרַ֨ע שָׁכַ֧ב כַּאֲרִ֛י וּכְלָבִ֖יא מִ֣י יְקִימֶ֑נּוּ מְבָרְכֶ֣יךָ בָר֔וּךְ וְאֹרְרֶ֖יךָ אָרֽוּר׃

They crouch, they lie down like a lion,
Like a lioness; who dares rouse them?
Blessed are they who bless you,
Cursed they who curse you!

Rashi on Numbers 23:24
BEHOLD, THE PEOPLE RISES AS A LIONESS, etc. — When they rise from their sleep in the morning they show themselves strong as a lioness and as a lion to "snatch at" the Divine precepts (to perform them immediately) — to clothe themselves with the Tallith, to read the Shema and to lay Tephillin (cf. Midrash Tanchuma, Balak 14).

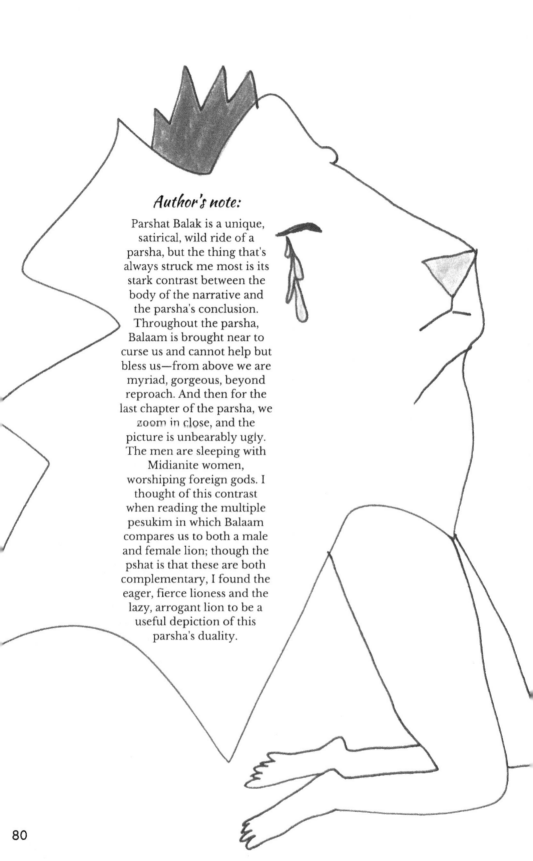

Author's note:

Parshat Balak is a unique, satirical, wild ride of a parsha, but the thing that's always struck me most is its stark contrast between the body of the narrative and the parsha's conclusion. Throughout the parsha, Balaam is brought near to curse us and cannot help but bless us—from above we are myriad, gorgeous, beyond reproach. And then for the last chapter of the parsha, we zoom in close, and the picture is unbearably ugly. The men are sleeping with Midianite women, worshiping foreign gods. I thought of this contrast when reading the multiple pesukim in which Balaam compares us to both a male and female lion; though the pshat is that these are both complementary, I found the eager, fierce lioness and the lazy, arrogant lion to be a useful depiction of this parsha's duality.

Pinchas

lama yigara memenu.
we too stood at
Sinai, awed and
trembling and holy
beside those who'd been
warned not to go near a
woman. when the
language erases us,
we are still there—
can you feel us crouching
beneath each pasuk?
can you feel the undercurrent
of our stories breathing
and stirring.

we were brilliant &
stubborn at Sinai, bangles
glinting on our folded
arms, earrings winking by
our cheeks, mouths
pursed in refusal as you
made your molten god.

we are brilliant &
victorious at the desert's
end, Eretz Yisrael just
beyond our line of sight.
your carcasses have
dropped in the desert,
but we stand tired and
erect.

the land is dear to us,
and we never once
looked back.

Numbers 14:29-30

בַּמִּדְבָּר הַזֶּה יִפְּלוּ פִגְרֵיכֶם וְכָל־פְּקֻדֵיכֶם לְכָל־מִסְפַּרְכֶם מִבֶּן עֶשְׂרִים שָׁנָה
וָמָעְלָה אֲשֶׁר הֲלִינֹתֶם עָלָי: אִם־אַתֶּם תָּבֹאוּ אֶל־הָאָרֶץ אֲשֶׁר נָשָׂאתִי אֶת־יָדִי
לְשַׁכֵּן אֶתְכֶם בָּהּ כִּי אִם־כָּלֵב בֶּן־יְפֻנֶּה וִיהוֹשֻׁעַ בִּן־נוּן:

In this very wilderness shall your carcasses drop. Of all of you [men]
who were recorded in your various lists from the age of twenty years
up, you who have muttered against Me, not one shall enter the land in
which I swore to settle you—
save Caleb son of Jephunneh and Joshua son of Nun.

Numbers 26:64

וּבְאֵלֶּה לֹא־הָיָה אִישׁ מִפְּקוּדֵי מֹשֶׁה וְאַהֲרֹן הַכֹּהֵן אֲשֶׁר פָּקְדוּ אֶת־בְּנֵי
יִשְׂרָאֵל בְּמִדְבַּר סִינָי:

Among these [in the census taken at the end of forty years] there was
not one of those enrolled by Moses and Aaron the priest when they
recorded the Israelites in the wilderness of Sinai.

Rashi on Numbers 26:64

BUT AMONG THESE THERE WAS NO MAN [OF THEM WHOM MOSES AND AARON
NUMBERED] — no man; but the decree consequent upon the incident of the spies [that no one over the age of
twenty should enter Eretz Yisrael] had not been enacted upon the women, because they held the Promised Land
dear. The men had said, (Numbers 14:4) "Let us appoint a chief and return to Egypt", while the women said,
(Numbers 27:4) "Give us a possession in the Land". On this account, too, the chapter regarding the daughters of
Zelophehad follows immediately here (Sifrei Bamidbar 133:1).

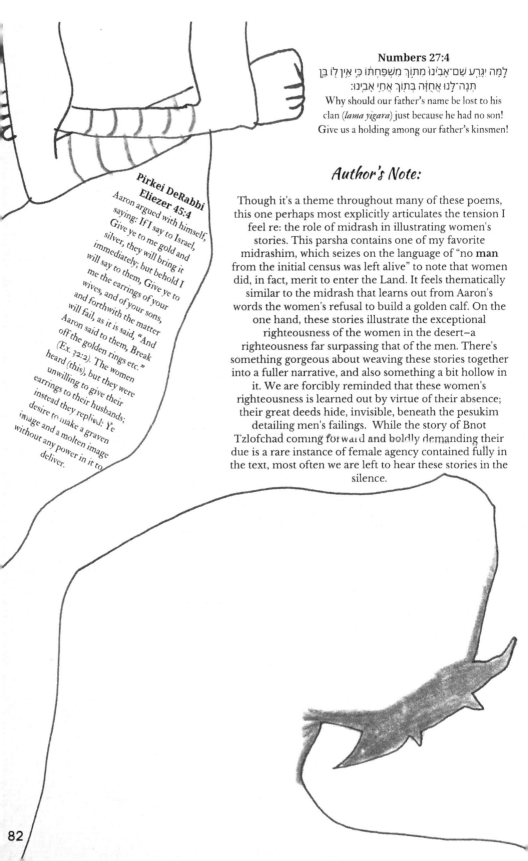

Numbers 27:4

לָמָּה יִגָּרַע שֵׁם־אָבִינוּ מִתּוֹךְ מִשְׁפַּחְתּוֹ כִּי אֵין לוֹ בֵּן
תְּנָה־לָּנוּ אֲחֻזָּה בְּתוֹךְ אֲחֵי אָבִינוּ:

Why should our father's name be lost to his
clan (*lama yigara*) just because he had no son!
Give us a holding among our father's kinsmen!

Author's Note:

Though it's a theme throughout many of these poems,
this one perhaps most explicitly articulates the tension I
feel re: the role of midrash in illustrating women's
stories. This parsha contains one of my favorite
midrashim, which seizes on the language of "no **man**
from the initial census was left alive" to note that women
did, in fact, merit to enter the Land. It feels thematically
similar to the midrash that learns out from Aaron's
words the women's refusal to build a golden calf. On the
one hand, these stories illustrate the exceptional
righteousness of the women in the desert—a
righteousness far surpassing that of the men. There's
something gorgeous about weaving these stories together
into a fuller narrative, and also something a bit hollow in
it. We are forcibly reminded that these women's
righteousness is learned out by virtue of their absence;
their great deeds hide, invisible, beneath the pesukim
detailing men's failings. While the story of Bnot
Tzlofchad coming forward and boldly demanding their
due is a rare instance of female agency contained fully in
the text, most often we are left to hear these stories in the
silence.

Pirkei DeRabbi Eliezer 45:4

Aaron argued with himself, saying: If I say to Israel, Give ye to me gold and silver, they will bring it immediately; but behold I will say to them, Give ye to me the earrings of your wives, and of your sons, and forthwith the matter will fail, as it is said, "And Aaron said to them, Break off the golden rings etc." (Ex. 32:2). The women heard (this), but they were unwilling to give their earrings to their husbands; instead they replied: Ye desire to make a graven image and a molten image without any power in it to deliver.

Mattot-Masei

we know that we have tested you—
have fought, bitterly,
cruelly—
have bitten the hand that feeds
us with relish—
have cast off every yoke only to
reassume it—
we know that you are old and weary
from years of bearing us in your arms
but we, we are not ready to let go.

drag us away, kicking and screaming.
we'll smile grimly as our enemies
fall from the sky;
they will not know we smile because
they keep coming.
fly closer, soldiers and gods—
we need just a little bit more time.

Numbers 11:14
לֹא־אוּכַל אָנֹכִי לְבַדִּי לָשֵׂאת אֶת־כָּל־הָעָם הַזֶּה כִּי
כָבֵד מִמֶּנִּי:
I shall not be able to bear alone all this people,
for it is beyond my strength.

Numbers 31:1-2
וַיְדַבֵּר יְהֹוָה אֶל־מֹשֶׁה לֵּאמֹר: נְקֹם נִקְמַת בְּנֵי
יִשְׂרָאֵל מֵאֵת הַמִּדְיָנִים אַחַר תֵּאָסֵף אֶל־עַמֶּיךָ:
Hashem spoke to Moses, saying, "Avenge the
Israelite people on the Midianites; then you
shall be gathered to your kin."

Numbers 31:5
וַיִּמָּסְרוּ מֵאַלְפֵי יִשְׂרָאֵל אֶלֶף לַמַּטֶּה
שְׁנֵים־עָשָׂר אֶלֶף חֲלוּצֵי צָבָא:
So a thousand from each tribe were
handed over from the divisions of Israel,
twelve thousand picked for the campaign
[against Midian].

Sifrei Bamidbar 157:3
R. Elazar Hamodai says:
Come and see the love (Israel
has) for the shepherd of Israel.
So long as they had not heard
that the death of Moses would
follow the war with Midian,
what is written of them?
(Exodus 17:4) "Just a little
more and they will stone me."
When they heard this, they
began hiding (to avoid
conscription, so as not to be
instrumental in his death) —
notwithstanding which they
were conscripted perforce, viz.
"And there were handed over
of the thousands of Israel,
etc." (Numbers 31:5).

Rashi on Numbers 31:6
AND THE VESSELS OF HOLINESS ... [WERE WITH
PINCHAS AND THE TROOPS] — these were the Ark and the
Golden Plate. Because Balaam was with the Midianites and through
enchantment he made the kings of Midian float in the air and he
himself floated with them, he (Phineas) held up to them the Golden
Plate upon which the Divine Name was engraved and they
immediately fell to the ground. On this account it is said (v. 8) of the
Kings of Midian that they were killed "upon those belonging to them
who had been killed," meaning that they fell from the air upon those
who had already been killed.

Rashi on Numbers 34:2
[THE LAND WHICH] FALLS
FOR YOU — A Midrashic
explanation of why this term is
employed here states: It is because
the Holy One, blessed be They, cast
down (lit., made fall) from heaven
the tutelary angels of the seven
nations of Canaan and placed them
in fetters before Moses, They said to
him, (Deuteronomy 1:21) "Behold
the Lord God hath put before thee
the tutelary angels of the land" —
there is no more strength in them.

Author's Note:

Continuing with the
theme of Moshe and
B'nei Yisrael's parent-
child relationship
(which will only
become more
prominent as we move
into Devarim), I found
the midrash of the
handed-over soldiers to
be particularly apt. The
parent is often a
presence to be
contended with or
resented so long as
they're around; but
only when threatened
with their loss does the
child recognize the
deep love and reliance
lying beneath all the
strife. They beg for the
parent to go, until the
parent finally does—at
which point they beg
them back. They have
been cruel to Moshe,
but they cannot
imagine what it is to
live without him.

Devarim

God knows
I've led you long enough
wandered with you, carried you
I led your parents
up to their land
but they saw giants
and would not go.

You were children then
and now you are old
so turn north
you've waited long enough
I've lived long enough
it is your time
to go.

Deuteronomy 2:3
רַב־לָכֶם סֹב אֶת־הָהָר הַזֶּה
פְּנוּ לָכֶם צָפֹנָה:
You have been skirting
this hill country long
enough; now turn
north!

maybe I can say it all again and
this time—
finally—
you'll hear me?

maybe I can say it all again and
you'll bow your heads, all
sad deferential & grateful,

you'll know what I have
sacrificed for you.

God sees you from above
but I see you from within and
you are so much dirtier and
lovelier than They know.

maybe this time,
with my own words,
they'll reach beyond this
ephemeral glowing veil and
you'll see that I am human,

that I am just human,
just like you.

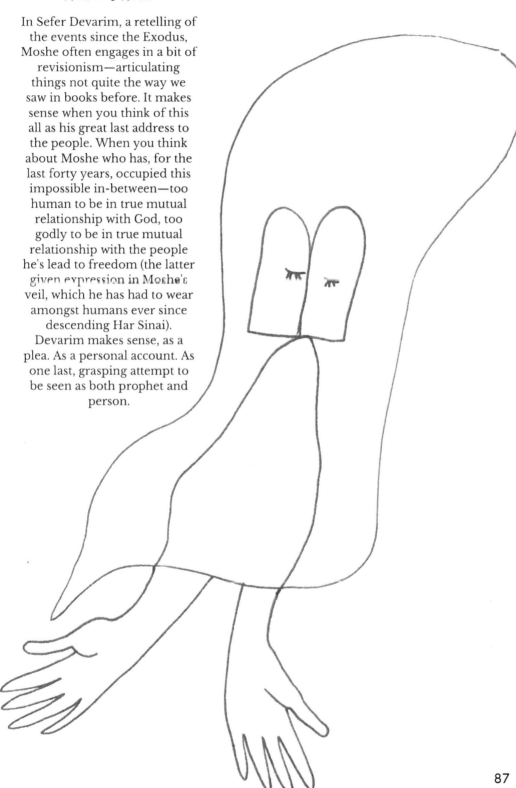

Author's Note:

In Sefer Devarim, a retelling of the events since the Exodus, Moshe often engages in a bit of revisionism—articulating things not quite the way we saw in books before. It makes sense when you think of this all as his great last address to the people. When you think about Moshe who has, for the last forty years, occupied this impossible in-between—too human to be in true mutual relationship with God, too godly to be in true mutual relationship with the people he's lead to freedom (the latter given expression in Moshe's veil, which he has had to wear amongst humans ever since descending Har Sinai). Devarim makes sense, as a plea. As a personal account. As one last, grasping attempt to be seen as both prophet and person.

it wasn't long before you became
too much for me to bear, squirming &
reckless & sometimes heavy as a stone,
but They scooped you up and set you on
Their back, your arms wrapped round Their
neck and feet kicking at Their sides and eyes
peeking, curious, above Their hairline,

They had nursed you to this life and now
would carry you through it, shielding your
unruly frail body with Their own,

but you slipped out of Their hold, toddled
off defiantly towards hazy distant figures,
so convinced Their arms were captivity and
not carrying that you imagined in Them the
same resentments you bore,

and I tried to catch at your hand, to lead
you when I could not hold you, to redirect
your wandering feet, but you tore your
hand from mine and veered away,

and when you came back tired confused &
bruised, with a face that looked almost
repentant, They locked you in your room
and leaned against the door, fingers perched
wearily on Their forehead. you beat at the
door and wept bitterly—alternately insisting
that your ways had changed, that you could
be good if only we let you, and cursing Them for
having ever let you leave the womb. the more
wretched you sound the more Their face quivers,

but They will not give in so easily. They may be
quick to forgive and scoop you back up in Their
arms, but you are slow to learn, and the fact is that
you must. the fact is we won't always chase after
you each time you run away. if you don't learn,
you may stay lost and wandering. and so They lean
against the door, weary and sorry and certain;

They lift their eyes to me, clasped hands and drawn
face at the hallway's end, and shake Their head. I
could not carry you, but perhaps I could've grasped
your hand tighter, given it one soft squeeze to say *hello,
I am here with you, and we will find our way.*

Author's Note:
Hashem and Moshe go through some
painful co-parenting. In the imagery of
tanakh and midrash, we see Hashem
occupy the roles both of nursing
mother and distant father.

Va'etchanan

rav lekha,

why do you think me keeping
your foot from this soil means
I love you less. why plead for
this imagined redemption. was
not this your redemption: my
voice thundering through you,
my eyelashes kissing your cheek
as you hid behind the rock. tent
flaps blowing open to welcome you
in, further in. you spent forty years
wandering and I loved you; you
carried the Torah on your lips, in
your veins, and I loved you. come,
like the Leviathan, and play with
me. we are holy wanderers, we are
holy in our wandering. *rav lekha,*
why cry over a border when I've
given you the whole world.

Deuteronomy 3:23-26

וָאֶתְחַנַּ֣ן אֶל־יְהֹוָ֔ה בָּעֵ֥ת הַהִ֖וא לֵאמֹֽר: אֲדֹנָ֣י
יֱהֹוִ֗ה אַתָּ֤ה הַחִלּ֙וֹתָ֙ לְהַרְא֣וֹת אֶֽת־עַבְדְּךָ֔
אֶ֨ת־גׇּדְלְךָ֔ וְאֶת־יָדְךָ֖ הַחֲזָקָ֑ה אֲשֶׁ֤ר מִי־אֵל֙
בַּשָּׁמַ֣יִם וּבָאָ֔רֶץ אֲשֶׁר־יַעֲשֶׂ֥ה כְמַעֲשֶׂ֖יךָ
וְכִגְבוּרֹתֶֽךָ: אֶעְבְּרָה־נָּ֗א וְאֶרְאֶה֙ אֶת־הָאָ֣רֶץ
הַטּוֹבָ֔ה אֲשֶׁ֖ר בְּעֵ֣בֶר הַיַּרְדֵּ֑ן הָהָ֥ר הַטּ֛וֹב
הַזֶּ֖ה וְהַלְּבָנֹֽן: וַיִּתְעַבֵּ֨ר יְהֹוָ֥ה בִּ֙י לְמַעַנְכֶ֔ם
וְלֹ֥א שָׁמַ֖ע אֵלָ֑י וַיֹּ֨אמֶר יְהֹוָ֤ה אֵלַי֙ רַב־לָ֔ךְ
אַל־תּ֗וֹסֶף דַּבֵּ֥ר אֵלַ֛י ע֖וֹד בַּדָּבָ֥ר הַזֶּֽה:

I pleaded with Hashem at that time,
saying, "O lord Hashem, You who let
Your servant see the first works of
Your greatness and Your mighty hand,
You whose powerful deeds no god in
heaven or on earth can equal! Let me, I
pray, cross over and see the good land
on the other side of the Jordan, that
good hill country, and the Lebanon."
But Hashem was wrathful with me on
your account and would not listen to
me. Hashem said to me, "Enough (*rav
lekha*)! Never speak to Me of this
matter again!"

Malbim on Deuteronomy 3:26

Rav lekha, enough–that is to say, you
already have perfection and holiness
that is not only sufficient but more
than sufficient; there is no additional
level remaining for you, to attain by
entering Eretz Yisrael.

Avodah Zarah 3b

The day consists of
twelve hours... During
the fourth [set of three
hours], God sits and
plays with Leviathan,
as it says, "There is
Leviathan, whom you
formed to play with."
(Psalms 104:26)

Rabbeinu Bahya on Deuteronomy 3:23

In a midrash on "And I pleaded," it envisions Moses saying to G'd: "You have
called me 'servant,' seeing You have said to Miriam and Aaron: 'not so My
servant Moses' (Numbers 12,7). I am Your servant and Leviathan is Your
servant. I am pleading with You and Leviathan is pleading with You...You
have accepted the pleadings of Leviathan [why else would Job be unable to
catch the Leviathan?] Moses continues: "Leviathan apparently has made a
covenant with You to remain Your lifelong slave." Moses argued that seeing
G'd had also said to him that They had made a covenant with him (Exodus
34,10), why should G'd listen any less to his entreaty than to that of the
Leviathan?

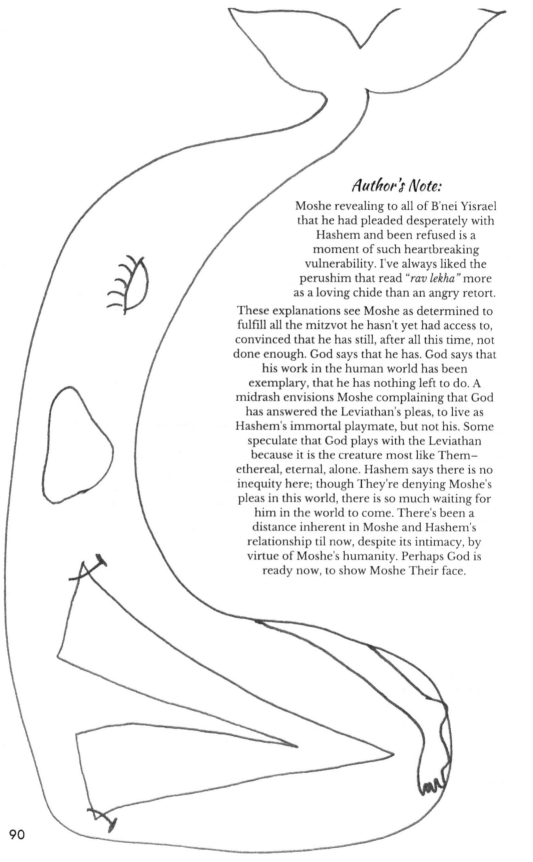

Author's Note:

Moshe revealing to all of B'nei Yisrael
that he had pleaded desperately with
Hashem and been refused is a
moment of such heartbreaking
vulnerability. I've always liked the
perushim that read *"rav lekha"* more
as a loving chide than an angry retort.

These explanations see Moshe as determined to
fulfill all the mitzvot he hasn't yet had access to,
convinced that he has still, after all this time, not
done enough. God says that he has. God says that
his work in the human world has been
exemplary, that he has nothing left to do. A
midrash envisions Moshe complaining that God
has answered the Leviathan's pleas, to live as
Hashem's immortal playmate, but not his. Some
speculate that God plays with the Leviathan
because it is the creature most like Them–
ethereal, eternal, alone. Hashem says there is no
inequity here; though They're denying Moshe's
pleas in this world, there is so much waiting for
him in the world to come. There's been a
distance inherent in Moshe and Hashem's
relationship til now, despite its intimacy, by
virtue of Moshe's humanity. Perhaps God is
ready now, to show Moshe Their face.

Ekev

press my garments fresh clean
new, I breathe in and know
I cannot live without you, I
breathe in smell detergent feel
stiff cotton I think that I have spent
forty years feeling so clean so clean
so clean, when I was three I stumbled
to the very edge of Korach's hole teetered—
and collapsed back in the dust, I choked
on dirt and ash and I woke the next day in
clothes the cleanest, cleanest, cleanest
white, the cloth was stiff around me as a
shell solid as a home hard and sure as a home
carried on my back forty years wandering,
wandering, you say we will build houses but
this shirt is my only notion of permanence, I
do not know how to live in place, do not
know how to make a home outside myself,
cannot imagine what the goodbye will feel
like that day I finally peel this shirt off and
slip into a tunic of crisp white linen that my
sister cleaned, down by the river.

Deuteronomy 8:4
שִׂמְלָתְךָ לֹא בָלְתָה מֵעָלֶיךָ
וְרַגְלְךָ לֹא בָצֵקָה זֶה אַרְבָּעִים
שָׁנָה:
The clothes upon you did not
wear out, nor did your feet
swell these forty years.

Shir HaShirim Rabbah 4:11
THY RAIMENT DID NOT WEAR OUT — the clouds of Divine Glory used to rub
the dirt off their clothes, bleach and iron them so that they looked like new white articles;
and also, the children, as they grew, their clothes grew with them, just like the clothes (shell)
of a snail which grows with it.

Re'eh

when they asked me why I came
to Jerusalem, wrong answers only,
I said that I have never been a fan of
traveling—that I find myself inexorably
bound to one place by maybe laziness
maybe dread maybe love, so when the
third beit hamikdash is built and the time
comes to eat our ma'aser sheni within the
city walls, to ascend three times a year and
rejoice and marvel before our Lord our G-d
I will be here, rooted and curious and patiently
waiting; when the young men come eager and
thronging through our gates, I will be perched on
a balcony with plenty in my lap and pomegranate
juice staining my chin. I will cross my legs twine
strings around my fingers look at You and say, *I
know you called for* kol zekhurekha *but I am
already here, I am already here.*

Deuteronomy 14:22-23
עַשֵּׂר תְּעַשֵּׂר אֵת כָּל־תְּבוּאַת
זַרְעֶךָ הַיֹּצֵא הַשָּׂדֶה שָׁנָה שָׁנָה:
וְאָכַלְתָּ לִפְנֵי | יְהוָה אֱלֹהֶיךָ
בַּמָּקוֹם אֲשֶׁר־יִבְחַר לְשַׁכֵּן שְׁמוֹ
שָׁם מַעְשַׂר דְּגָנְךָ תִּירֹשְׁךָ
וְיִצְהָרֶךָ וּבְכֹרֹת בְּקָרְךָ וְצֹאנֶךָ
לְמַעַן תִּלְמַד לְיִרְאָה אֶת־יְהוָה
אֱלֹהֶיךָ כָּל־הַיָּמִים:

You shall set aside every year a
tenth part of all the yield of
your sowing that is brought
from the field. You shall
consume the tithes of your
new grain and wine and oil,
and the firstlings of your
herds and flocks, in the
presence of your God
Hashem, in the place where
[God] will choose to establish
the divine name, so that you
may learn to revere your God
Hashem forever.

Deuteronomy 16:16
שָׁלוֹשׁ פְּעָמִים | בַּשָּׁנָה יֵרָאֶה כָל־זְכוּרְךָ
אֶת־פְּנֵי | יְהוָה אֱלֹהֶיךָ בַּמָּקוֹם אֲשֶׁר יִבְחָר
בְּחַג הַמַּצּוֹת וּבְחַג הַשָּׁבֻעוֹת וּבְחַג הַסֻּכּוֹת וְלֹא
יֵרָאֶה אֶת־פְּנֵי יְהוָה רֵיקָם:

Three times a year—on the Feast of
Unleavened Bread, on the Feast of Weeks,
and on the Feast of Booths—all your males
(*kol zekhurekha*) shall appear before your
God Hashem in the place that [God] will
choose. They shall not appear before
Hashem empty-handed...

Author's Note:

In some texts, like
those associated
with the *regalim*,
the language of "all
your males" is
explicit. In others,
it instructs you to
bring your
household—your
daughters, sons,
slaves, and
Levites—but not
your wife.

when I whisper words to you all sweet and
seductive, all casual care and gentle persuasion,
you cannot kill me for it. when you follow me,
gladly, thoughtlessly, it will feel like falling.
you'll never regain your feet. I suppose you're
not worried about a temptress—suppose you think
you've learned from Adam. when your city is
reduced to death & ashes, you'll have only yourselves
to blame.

Deuteronomy 13:13-17

כִּי־תִשְׁמַ֞ע בְּאַחַ֣ת עָרֶ֗יךָ אֲשֶׁר֩ יְהֹוָ֨ה אֱלֹהֶ֜יךָ נֹתֵ֥ן לְךָ֛ לָשֶׁ֥בֶת שָׁ֖ם לֵאמֹֽר׃ יָצְא֞וּ אֲנָשִׁ֤ים בְּנֵֽי־בְלִיַּ֙עַל֙ מִקִּרְבֶּ֔ךָ
וַיַּדִּ֛יחוּ אֶת־יֹשְׁבֵ֥י עִירָ֖ם לֵאמֹ֑ר נֵֽלְכָ֗ה וְנַֽעַבְדָ֛ה אֱלֹהִ֥ים אֲחֵרִ֖ים אֲשֶׁ֥ר לֹֽא־יְדַעְתֶּֽם׃ וְדָרַשְׁתָּ֧ וְחָקַרְתָּ֛ וְשָׁאַלְתָּ֖
הֵיטֵ֑ב וְהִנֵּ֤ה אֱמֶת֙ נָכ֣וֹן הַדָּבָ֔ר נֶעֶשְׂתָ֛ה הַתּוֹעֵבָ֥ה הַזֹּ֖את בְּקִרְבֶּֽךָ׃ הַכֵּ֣ה תַכֶּ֗ה אֶת־יֹֽשְׁבֵ֛י הָעִ֥יר הַהִ֖וא
לְפִי־חָ֑רֶב הַחֲרֵ֣ם אֹתָ֣הּ וְאֶת־כָּל־אֲשֶׁר־בָּ֛הּ וְאֶת־בְּהֶמְתָּ֖הּ לְפִי־חָֽרֶב׃ וְאֶת־כָּל־שְׁלָלָ֗הּ תִּקְבֹּץ֮ אֶל־תּ֣וֹךְ
רְחֹבָהּ֒ וְשָׂרַפְתָּ֨ בָאֵ֜שׁ אֶת־הָעִ֤יר וְאֶת־כָּל־שְׁלָלָהּ֙ כָּלִ֔יל לַיהֹוָ֖ה אֱלֹהֶ֑יךָ וְהָיְתָה֙ תֵּ֣ל עוֹלָ֔ם לֹ֥א תִבָּנֶ֖ה עֽוֹד׃

If you hear it said, of one of the towns that your God Hashem is giving you to dwell in, that
some men of no morals from among you have gone and subverted the inhabitants of their town,
saying, "Come let us worship other gods"—whom you have not experienced—you shall
investigate and inquire and interrogate thoroughly. If it is true, the fact is established—that
abhorrent thing was perpetrated in your midst—put the inhabitants of that town to the sword
and put its cattle to the sword. Doom it and all that is in it to destruction: gather all its spoil into
the open square, and burn the town and all its spoil as a holocaust to your God Hashem. And it
shall remain an everlasting ruin, never to be rebuilt.

Sifrei Devarim 93:1

"Some men have gone out"—men, but not women.

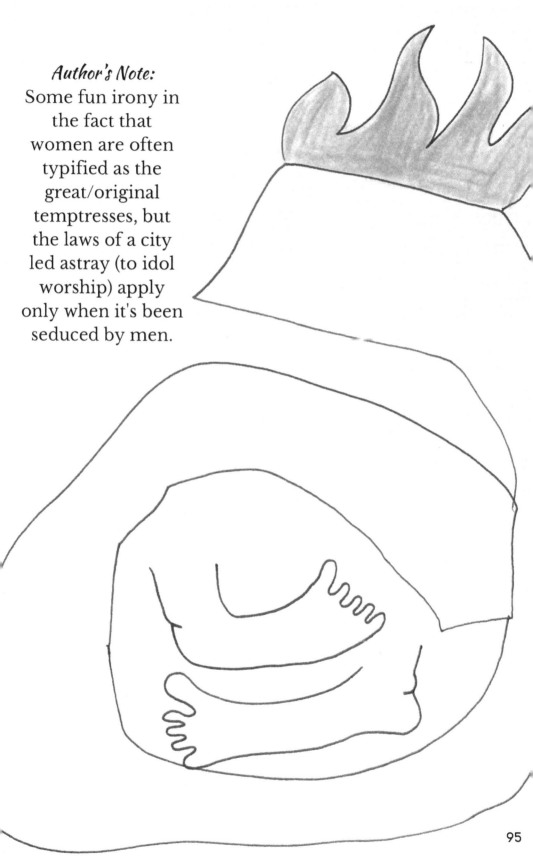

Author's Note:
Some fun irony in the fact that women are often typified as the great/original temptresses, but the laws of a city led astray (to idol worship) apply only when it's been seduced by men.

Shoftim

be perfect with the lord your G-d
be perfect with G-d be perfect, G-d
& I swear I will prophesy only bad
things so you can avert them so you
can see us imperfect and striving for
perfection so you can see that our
faith is fragile and immense so that
you can be perfect even when we are
not.

Deuteronomy 18:13

תָּמִים תִּהְיֶה עִם יְהֹוָה אֱלֹהֶיךָ:

You must be perfect with the Lord your God.

Deuteronomy 18:20-22

אַךְ הַנָּבִיא אֲשֶׁר יָזִיד לְדַבֵּר דָּבָר בִּשְׁמִי אֵת אֲשֶׁר לֹא־צִוִּיתִיו לְדַבֵּר וַאֲשֶׁר יְדַבֵּר בְּשֵׁם אֱלֹהִים אֲחֵרִים וּמֵת הַנָּבִיא הַהוּא: וְכִי תֹאמַר בִּלְבָבֶךָ אֵיכָה נֵדַע אֶת־הַדָּבָר אֲשֶׁר לֹא־דִבְּרוֹ יְהֹוָה: אֲשֶׁר יְדַבֵּר הַנָּבִיא בְּשֵׁם יְהֹוָה וְלֹא־יִהְיֶה הַדָּבָר וְלֹא יָבֹא הוּא הַדָּבָר אֲשֶׁר לֹא־דִבְּרוֹ יְהֹוָה בְּזָדוֹן דִּבְּרוֹ הַנָּבִיא לֹא תָגוּר מִמֶּנּוּ:

But any prophet who presumes to speak in My name an oracle that I did not command to be uttered, or who speaks in the name of other gods—that prophet shall die. And should you ask yourselves, "How can we know that the oracle was not spoken by Hashem?" if the prophet speaks in the name of Hashem and the oracle does not come true, that oracle was not spoken by Hashem; the prophet has uttered it presumptuously: do not stand in dread of that person.

Mishneh Torah, Foundations of the Torah 10:5

Concerning a prophet's prediction of calamities, i.e. such one would die, or such year would be visited by famine, or war, or matters similar to these, even though her words be not established, it is not considered contradictory to her prophecy. It shall not be said: "Behold, she spoke and it did not come to pass!" For, the Holy One, blessed is They! is long-suffering and abundant in goodness, and repenteth Them of the evil, and it is possible that the people repented and were forgiven, as did the inhabitants of Nineveh,or that their fate was postponed, as was with Hezekiah. But if she assured that good would come to pass, saying that it would be thus and such, but the good she promised did not come to pass, it is certain that she is a false prophet, for every good thing God decides upon, even though it be contingent, They do not change Their mind.

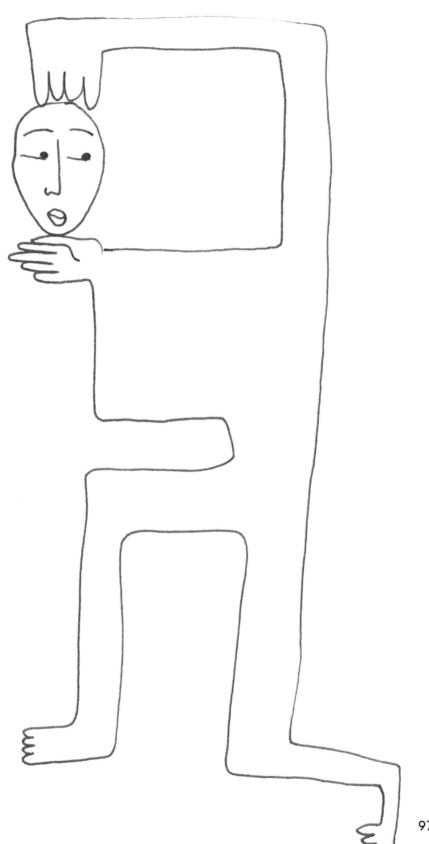

Ki Tetze

she waits in the corner
of the field, she gathers
the forgotten grapes.
she will not be borrowed
nor claimed by another
her clothes are her own
and she spits in their face.
a widow gleans
where she will.

> **Deuteronomy 24:21**
>
> כִּי תִבְצֹר כַּרְמְךָ לֹא תְעוֹלֵל אַחֲרֶיךָ לַגֵּר
> לַיָּתוֹם וְלָאַלְמָנָה יִהְיֶה:
>
> When you gather the grapes of your
> vineyard, do not pick it over again;
> that shall go to the stranger, the
> fatherless, and the widow.

at sundown you passed
by him and said, I think
I found your soul & shoes
lying by the side of the road,
can you prove these are yours?
and his face looked down at you,
G-d's face looked down at you,
his bare feet swung in the wind &
you nodded with them, said "oh,
god, I knew you were guilty" and
blew back his soul with a kiss

Deuteronomy 21:22-23

וְכִי־יִהְיֶה בְאִישׁ חֵטְא מִשְׁפַּט־מָוֶת וְהוּמָת וְתָלִיתָ אֹתוֹ
עַל־עֵץ: לֹא־תָלִין נִבְלָתוֹ עַל־הָעֵץ כִּי־קָבוֹר תִּקְבְּרֶנּוּ בַּיּוֹם
הַהוּא כִּי־קִלְלַת אֱלֹהִים תָּלוּי וְלֹא תְטַמֵּא אֶת־אַדְמָתְךָ
אֲשֶׁר יְהוָה אֱלֹהֶיךָ נֹתֵן לְךָ נַחֲלָה:

If any party is guilty of a capital offense and is put to
death, and you impale the body on a stake, you must
not let the corpse remain on the stake overnight, but
must bury it the same day. For an impaled body is an
affront to God: you shall not defile the land that
your God יהוה is giving you to possess.

Rashi on Deuteronomy 21:23
FOR HE THAT IS HANGED IS A קללת
אלהים — i.e., a degradation of the Divine
King, for man is made in His image and the
Israelites are His children. A parable! It may
be compared to the case of two twin brothers
who very closely resembled each other: one
became king and the other was arrested for
robbery and was hanged. Whoever saw him
on the gallows thought that the king was
hanged (Sanhedrin 46b).

Deuteronomy 22:1-3

וַאֲסַפְתּוֹ אֶל־תּוֹךְ בֵּיתֶךָ וְהָיָה עִמְּךָ עַד דְּרֹשׁ אָחִיךָ אֹתוֹ ...
וַהֲשֵׁבֹתוֹ לוֹ: וְכֵן תַּעֲשֶׂה לַחֲמֹרוֹ וְכֵן תַּעֲשֶׂה לְשִׂמְלָתוֹ וְכֵן תַּעֲשֶׂה
לְכָל־אֲבֵדַת אָחִיךָ אֲשֶׁר־תֹּאבַד מִמֶּנּוּ וּמְצָאתָהּ לֹא תוּכַל
לְהִתְעַלֵּם:

...you shall bring [the lost object] home and it shall remain
with you until your peer claims it; then you shall give it
back. You shall do the same with that person's ass; you shall
do the same with that person's garment; and so too shall
you do with anything that your fellow Israelite loses and
you find: you must not remain indifferent.

Deuteronomy 25:8-10

וְקָרְאוּ־לוֹ זִקְנֵי־עִירוֹ וְדִבְּרוּ אֵלָיו וְעָמַד
וְאָמַר לֹא חָפַצְתִּי לְקַחְתָּהּ: וְנִגְּשָׁה
יְבִמְתּוֹ אֵלָיו לְעֵינֵי הַזְּקֵנִים וְחָלְצָה נַעֲלוֹ
מֵעַל רַגְלוֹ וְיָרְקָה בְּפָנָיו וְעָנְתָה וְאָמְרָה
כָּכָה יֵעָשֶׂה לָאִישׁ אֲשֶׁר לֹא־יִבְנֶה
אֶת־בֵּית אָחִיו: וְנִקְרָא שְׁמוֹ בְּיִשְׂרָאֵל
בֵּית חֲלוּץ הַנָּעַל:

The elders of his town shall then
summon him and talk to him. If he
insists, saying, "I do not want to take
her," his brother's widow shall go up
to him in the presence of the elders,
pull the sandal off his foot, spit in
his face, and make this declaration:
Thus shall be done to the man who
will not build up his brother's
house! And he shall go in Israel by
the name of "the family of the
unsandaled one."

Author's Note:
This poem is a jumble of images and
instructions from the parsha. The
commandment to return lost objects; the
slightly absurd image of the unsandaled
yavam; and the prohibition of leaving a
corpse out overnight, lest you see their
face in the morning light, that face made
in the divine image, and think we've tried
& convicted God.

Ki Tavo

breathe sanctity into her sweetly & sincerely,
water her with Torah and she'll bring forth for
you blossoms—you'll tie their fruits and cry out
"behold! what we have made, together" and they
will be the first of many; maybe they will appear
so beautifully, so regularly that you begin believing
she will always blossom for you. maybe you'll even
decide you could tear these from the ground yourself,
sweet and fleshy and fully-birthed.

Deuteronomy 26:1-2

וְהָיָה כִּי־תָבוֹא אֶל־הָאָרֶץ אֲשֶׁר יְהוָה אֱלֹהֶיךָ נֹתֵן לְךָ נַחֲלָה
וִירִשְׁתָּהּ וְיָשַׁבְתָּ בָּהּ: וְלָקַחְתָּ מֵרֵאשִׁית | כָּל־פְּרִי הָאֲדָמָה
אֲשֶׁר תָּבִיא מֵאַרְצְךָ אֲשֶׁר יְהוָה אֱלֹהֶיךָ נֹתֵן לָךְ וְשַׂמְתָּ
בַטֶּנֶא וְהָלַכְתָּ אֶל־הַמָּקוֹם אֲשֶׁר יִבְחַר יְהוָה אֱלֹהֶיךָ לְשַׁכֵּן
שְׁמוֹ שָׁם:

When you enter the land that your God Hashem is
giving you as a heritage, and you possess it and settle in
it, you shall take some of every first fruit of the soil,
which you harvest from the land that your God
Hashem is giving you, put it in a basket and go to the
place where your God Hashem will choose to establish
the divine name.

Mishna Bikkurim 3:1

How does one set aside
bikkurim (first fruits)? A
man goes down into his
field, he sees a fig that
ripened, or a cluster of
grapes that ripened, or a
pomegranate that ripened,
he ties a reed-rope around it
and says: "Let these be
bikkurim."

Deuteronomy 28:15,30

וְהָיָה אִם־לֹא תִשְׁמַע בְּקוֹל יְהוָה אֱלֹהֶיךָ לִשְׁמֹר לַעֲשׂוֹת אֶת־כָּל־מִצְוֺתָיו וְחֻקֹּתָיו אֲשֶׁר אָנֹכִי מְצַוְּךָ הַיּוֹם
וּבָאוּ עָלֶיךָ כָּל־הַקְּלָלוֹת הָאֵלֶּה וְהִשִּׂיגוּךָ:...אִשָּׁה תְאָרֵשׂ וְאִישׁ אַחֵר (ישגלנה) [יִשְׁכָּבֶנָּה] בַּיִת תִּבְנֶה
וְלֹא־תֵשֵׁב בּוֹ כֶּרֶם תִּטַּע וְלֹא תְחַלְּלֶנּוּ:

But if you do not obey your God Hashem to observe faithfully all the commandments and laws
which I enjoin upon you this day, all these curses shall come upon you and take effect: ...If you [a
man] pay the bride-price for a wife, another man shall enjoy her. If you build a house, you shall
not live in it. If you plant a vineyard, you shall not harvest it.

Deuteronomy 8:12-14,17

פֶּן־תֹּאכַל וְשָׂבָעְתָּ וּבָתִּים טֹבִים תִּבְנֶה
וְיָשָׁבְתָּ: וּבְקָרְךָ וְצֹאנְךָ יִרְבְּיֻן וְכֶסֶף וְזָהָב
יִרְבֶּה־לָּךְ וְכֹל אֲשֶׁר־לְךָ יִרְבֶּה: וְרָם
לְבָבֶךָ וְשָׁכַחְתָּ אֶת־יְהוָה אֱלֹהֶיךָ
הַמּוֹצִיאֲךָ מֵאֶרֶץ מִצְרַיִם מִבֵּית עֲבָדִים:
...וְאָמַרְתָּ בִּלְבָבֶךָ כֹּחִי וְעֹצֶם יָדִי עָשָׂה
לִי אֶת־הַחַיִל הַזֶּה:

When you have eaten your fill, and
have built fine houses to live in, and
your herds and flocks have
multiplied, and your silver and gold
have increased, and everything you
own has prospered,
beware lest your heart grow haughty
and you forget your God Hashem...
and you say to yourselves, "My own
power and the might of my own
hand have won this wealth for me."

Author's Note:

The process of identifying one's bikkurim is
both triumphant and humble—a sort of pride
in their emergence, followed by the offering to
Hashem, the acknowledgment that this is
ultimately neither ours to own nor solely the
product of our labor. It reminded me of one of
the *klallot* (curses) later in the parsha, where
another man "enjoying" your wife is compared
to another person harvesting your vineyard; in
both cases, you are unable to enjoy the fruits of
your labor, the production of your property.
Hashem notes earlier on that the people's
inevitable corruption, their future rebellion, is
likely to emerge from a sense of abundance—
that people grow comfortable with their riches,
and grow surer and surer that these riches have
come through nothing but their own merit.

Nitzavim

you are standing here this day,
all of you,
for the last time—
breathe in, look around.
lower your head and feel your
great-great-great-granddaughter's
breath tickling your neck.
look around at your proud, huddled

masses.

you are standing here this day,
to hear Torah you will only ever
live by half.

when this is over, when you have
heard the Torah that is not in Heaven,
you will stumble away like calves,
learning to walk on solid ground.

Deuteronomy 29:9-14

אַתֶּם נִצָּבִים הַיּוֹם כֻּלְּכֶם לִפְנֵי יְהֹוָה
אֱלֹהֵיכֶם רָאשֵׁיכֶם שִׁבְטֵיכֶם זִקְנֵיכֶם
וְשֹׁטְרֵיכֶם כֹּל אִישׁ יִשְׂרָאֵל: טַפְּכֶם נְשֵׁיכֶם
וְגֵרְךָ אֲשֶׁר בְּקֶרֶב מַחֲנֶיךָ מֵחֹטֵב עֵצֶיךָ עַד
שֹׁאֵב מֵימֶיךָ: לְעׇבְרְךָ בִּבְרִית יְהֹוָה אֱלֹהֶיךָ
וּבְאָלָתוֹ אֲשֶׁר יְהֹוָה אֱלֹהֶיךָ כֹּרֵת עִמְּךָ הַיּוֹם:
לְמַעַן הָקִים־אֹתְךָ הַיּוֹם | לוֹ לְעָם וְהוּא
יִהְיֶה־לְּךָ לֵאלֹהִים כַּאֲשֶׁר דִּבֶּר־לָךְ וְכַאֲשֶׁר
נִשְׁבַּע לַאֲבֹתֶיךָ לְאַבְרָהָם לְיִצְחָק וּלְיַעֲקֹב:
וְלֹא אִתְּכֶם לְבַדְּכֶם אָנֹכִי כֹּרֵת אֶת־הַבְּרִית
הַזֹּאת וְאֶת־הָאָלָה הַזֹּאת: כִּי אֶת־אֲשֶׁר יֶשְׁנוֹ
פֹּה עִמָּנוּ עֹמֵד הַיּוֹם לִפְנֵי יְהֹוָה אֱלֹהֵינוּ וְאֵת
אֲשֶׁר אֵינֶנּוּ פֹּה עִמָּנוּ הַיּוֹם:

You stand this day, all of you, before your
God יהוה —your tribal heads, your
elders, and your officials, every
householder in Israel, your children, your
wives, even the stranger within your
camp, from woodchopper to waterdrawer
—to enter into the covenant of your God
יהוה, which your God יהוה is concluding
with you this day, with its sanctions; in
order to establish you this day as God's
people and in order to be your God, as
promised you and as sworn to your
fathers Abraham, Isaac, and Jacob. I
make this covenant, with its sanctions,
not with you alone, but both with those
who are standing here with us this day
before our God יהוה and with those who
are not with us here this day.

Chizkuni on Deuteornomy 29:11
"The covenant...which They conclude with you
this day." No one can ever claim that she had not
been present at that time and had not confirmed
accepting the covenant. This was the last time
the entire nation would be present at the same
spot simultaneously, as the tribes living on the
other side of the Jordan would soon split off, and
after the land had been distributed to the tribes,
the elderly and the mothers who had just given
birth, as well as any sick people, could not be
expected to come to Jerusalem on the festivals
designated for the annual pilgrimages.

Midrash Tanchuma, Pekudei 3:4
You should know that every soul, from Adam to
the end of the world, was formed during the six
days of creation, and that all of them were present
in the Garden of Eden and at the time of the
giving of the Torah, as it is said: With those that
standeth here with us this day, and also with tbose
that are not here with us this day (Deut. 29:14).

Tosafot Gittin 36a

...in the time of the Second Temple they did not keep the Yovel (the Jubilee), as not all of the land's inhabitants were upon it, and thus Shmita (the Sabbatical Year) was only kept as a rabbinic-level mitzvah.

Author's Note:

If the speech in Parshat Nitzavim is the last time— not only in tanakh, but all of history—that the entire people of Israel is gathered together, and the laws of Yovel and Shmitta only apply on a Torah-level when the whole people (minimally all 12 tribes) is in the land, then Hashem directly commanded us with mitzvot that have never been fulfilled beyond a d'rabanan level. That's a wild concept!

Vayelekh

we are here because
we are here because
we are here because
we are here,
chazak v'ematz our love
will last far longer than
we do,
chazak v'ematz I can't
have done enough but
I am done,

you will fail and you
will return.
she knew from the
moment she made you
that you'd fail and yet,
she cast down truth to
breathe life into your
nostrils,
tentative and hopeful.

you will fail and she
will fail and you will
return to one another,
stepping with joy into
the fullness of what you
might, someday, be.

Clyde Cremer, "The Life and Times of a World War I Soldier"
British soldiers in World War I trenches sang "We're Here Because We're Here"
to the tune of "Auld Lang Syne".

Deuteronomy 31:16

וַיֹּאמֶר יְהֹוָה אֶל־מֹשֶׁה הִנְּךָ שֹׁכֵב עִם־אֲבֹתֶיךָ וְקָם֩ הָעָם֩ הַזֶּה וְזָנָה | אַחֲרֵי | אֱלֹהֵי
נֵכַר־הָאָרֶץ אֲשֶׁר הוּא בָא־שָׁמָּה בְּקִרְבּוֹ וַעֲזָבַנִי וְהֵפֵר אֶת־בְּרִיתִי אֲשֶׁר כָּרַתִּי אִתּוֹ:

Hashem said to Moses: You are soon to lie with your ancestors. This people will
thereupon go astray after the alien gods in their midst, in the land that they are
about to enter; they will forsake Me and break My covenant that I made with them.

Deuteronomy 31:19

וְעַתָּה כִּתְבוּ לָכֶם אֶת־הַשִּׁירָה הַזֹּאת וְלַמְּדָהּ אֶת־בְּנֵי־יִשְׂרָאֵל שִׂימָהּ בְּפִיהֶם לְמַעַן תִּהְיֶה־לִּי
הַשִּׁירָה הַזֹּאת לְעֵד בִּבְנֵי יִשְׂרָאֵל:

Therefore, write for yourselves this poem and teach it to the people of Israel; put it in
their mouths, in order that this poem may be My witness against the people of Israel.

Malbim on Deuteronomy 31:19

"Now write down for yourselves..." It seems this can be explained with a parable. A
queen redeemed a slave from jail and placed them in charge of her storehouses. The
queen knew this slave was a thief, knew that this was his nature, and that at some point
he would surely steal from the queen's storehouses and make himself liable for death.
The queen, who does not desire the slave's death, writes in her notebook a reminder
that it is the slave's nature to steal. One who saw this notebook would think she wrote
it as a warning such that if the slave steals he should be punished doubly; but
truthfully, this was a warning to the queen that if the slave should steal, he should not
be punished, as she knew this was his nature and nonetheless chose him. This is why
it's written, "I know today that in the future you will sin," and then it is written,
"Now write for yourselves this song," which will be for your benefit.

Author's Note:

The week of this parsha, I was listening to John Green's "The
Anthropocene Reviewed," in which he mentions the practice of
British soldiers to sing this nihilistic refrain in the trenches. He
says a friend of his had in a way reappropriated the song, and
would sing it at events—no longer as a declaration of pointlessness,
but as an affirmation. That even if what we accomplish is
incomplete or meaningless or forgotten, the love of that labor and
those relationships formed remain long after you're gone.

I thought of Moshe, tasked with comforting the people before his death, installing Joshua and
instilling their faith in him, only to be immediately told by God that following his death, they will
fail. They will not follow these laws. They will go astray. I thought of Hashem's commandment to
write the poem "Ha'azinu," and Malbim's interpretation that this is meant not as condemnation but
as salvation; as proof that Hashem knew we would fail, knew our flawed nature and accepted us
anyway (as seen in a midrash referenced earlier where Hashem cast down the protesting angel of
Truth in order to create humankind). I try to think of Moshe being told that his legacy will be
incomplete, imperfectly fulfilled, but he has still done good, and done enough. I imagine Hashem
reassuring him that the people will go astray, and They chose them anyway.

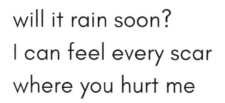

will it rain soon?
I can feel every scar
where you hurt me

sometimes I hide
until you believe
you'll never see me

I've known you so long
and now I hear your song
returning

I wrote this song for you
read it, and be strong
I can still hold you.

Midrash Tanchuma, Haazinu 3

וְלָמָה נִמְשְׁלָה תוֹרָה לְמָטָר. לוֹמַר, מַה מָטָר מַשְׁחֶקֶת אֲבָנִים, שֶׁנֶּאֱמַר: אֲבָנִים שָׁחֲקוּ מַיִם (איוב יד, יט), אַף הַתּוֹרָה מַשְׁחֶקֶת לֵב הָאֶבֶן.

And why is Torah compared to rain? To say that just as rain
erodes stones, as is written "water wears away stones"
[Job 14:19], so too Torah wears away a heart of stone.

Nitzavim-Vayelekh

it is not in heavens or across the sea, it isn't impossibly
far beyond your grasp it is here, in my hands—see how
I've spread them before you. my heart: see how it has unfolded
petal by petal these forty years, how I speak to you with love and
weariness, how I have strived and perhaps, sometimes, failed to
be better. take these words from me—I can no longer carry you,
that impossible weight, but I can gift to you these words, light as
a feather, that transfer from my palms to yours with the slightest
puff of air. look at this: it is in your grasp. to be good, to be good,
to listen and love and be good, it is in your grasp. I can almost see
double, see it sifting through your fingers like sand, but all I can do
is hope you cup these letters in your palms, gently; that even once I'm
gone, you'll hear the great earth-shattering call and return, you'll return.

Deuteronomy 30:11-15

כִּי הַמִּצְוָה הַזֹּאת אֲשֶׁר אָנֹכִי מְצַוְּךָ הַיּוֹם לֹא־נִפְלֵאת הִוא מִמְּךָ וְלֹא רְחֹקָה הִוא: לֹא בַשָּׁמַיִם הִוא לֵאמֹר מִי
יַעֲלֶה־לָּנוּ הַשָּׁמַיְמָה וְיִקָּחֶהָ לָּנוּ וְיַשְׁמִעֵנוּ אֹתָהּ וְנַעֲשֶׂנָּה: וְלֹא־מֵעֵבֶר לַיָּם הִוא לֵאמֹר מִי יַעֲבָר־לָנוּ אֶל־עֵבֶר
הַיָּם וְיִקָּחֶהָ לָּנוּ וְיַשְׁמִעֵנוּ אֹתָהּ וְנַעֲשֶׂנָּה: כִּי־קָרוֹב אֵלֶיךָ הַדָּבָר מְאֹד בְּפִיךָ וּבִלְבָבְךָ לַעֲשֹׂתוֹ: רְאֵה נָתַתִּי לְפָנֶיךָ
הַיּוֹם אֶת־הַחַיִּים וְאֶת־הַטּוֹב וְאֶת־הַמָּוֶת וְאֶת־הָרָע:

Surely, this Instruction which I enjoin upon you this day is not too baffling for you, nor is it beyond
reach. It is not in the heavens, that you should say, "Who among us can go up to the heavens and get
it for us and impart it to us, that we may observe it?" Neither is it beyond the sea, that you should say,
"Who among us can cross to the other side of the sea and get it for us and impart it to us, that we may
observe it?" No, the thing is very close to you, in your mouth and in your heart, to observe it. See, I
set before you this day life and good, death and adversity.

Kli Yakar on Deuteronomy 30:15

Life and the good. If it is life that you seek, look towards the good, to do that which
is good in the eyes of Hashem. And if you ask, why "good" is not mentioned first,
for it is through the good actions that one merits life, the answer is that it comes to
warn us not to do that which is good in Hashem's eyes only in order to live. But
rather to live in order to do that which is good.

Ha'azinu

I found you in the howling wastes gave
form to stubborn clay dangling *al bli-mah*
fought for you even when I knew I shouldn't
nursed you held you you clothed you anointed
you in oil and sent you off with a kiss on
your shining brows, knowing once you turned
away I'd never see your face again. when I see
you hurtling forward, all stiff-necked refusal and
bitter failure, Truth blooms vindicated from the
ground with a knowing frown and I chose you
because I cannot defend you; I'd never know you
loved me if I hadn't felt you loathe me, would never
treasure every sweet liberation if I hadn't seen the
howling wastes from which you wrested it.

Job 26:7
נֹטֶה צָפוֹן עַל־תֹּהוּ תֹּלֶה אֶרֶץ
עַל־בְּלִי־מָה:
It is They who stretched out
Tzaphon over chaos,
Who suspended earth over
emptiness (*al bli-mah*).

Deuteronomy 32:10
יִמְצָאֵהוּ בְּאֶרֶץ מִדְבָּר וּבְתֹהוּ יְלֵל יְשִׁמֹן יְסֹבְבֶנְהוּ יְבוֹנְנֵהוּ
יִצְּרֶנְהוּ כְּאִישׁוֹן עֵינוֹ:
God found them in a desert land,
In an empty howling waste,
[God] engirded them, watched over them,
Guarded them as the pupil of God's eye.

Ezekiel 16:8-9
וָאֶעֱבֹר עָלַיִךְ וָאֶרְאֵךְ וְהִנֵּה עִתֵּךְ עֵת דֹּדִים וָאֶפְרֹשׂ כְּנָפִי
עָלַיִךְ וָאֲכַסֶּה עֶרְוָתֵךְ וָאֶשָּׁבַע לָךְ וָאָבוֹא בִבְרִית אֹתָךְ נְאֻם
אֲדֹנָי יֱהוִה וַתִּהְיִי־לִי: וָאֶרְחָצֵךְ בַּמַּיִם וָאֶשְׁטֹף דָּמַיִךְ מֵעָלָיִךְ
וָאֲסֻכֵךְ בַּשָּׁמֶן:
When I passed by you [again in the wilderness] and saw
that your time for love had arrived, So I spread My robe
over you and covered your nakedness, and I entered into
a covenant with you by oath—declares the Lord GOD;
thus you became Mine. I bathed you in water, and
washed the blood off you, and anointed you with oil.

Zohar Atkins on Parshat Ha'Azinu, "Origins Are Not Destiny"
That phenomenon is not obedience, per se, which God can enforce through intimidation and coercion, but
willing obedience. Any God can be a despotic tyrant, but a covenantal God seeks to be a legitimate authority.
If God chooses a non-rebellious people, a non-stiff-necked people, God is not choosing relationship, but a
bot. The rebelliousness of Israel is a feature, not a bug...
Adorno suggests, much like Rebbe Nachman of Bratslav, that redemption can appear to us in a negative
light. Every time, we have a sense of injustice, a sense of failure and disappointment, a sense that this ain't it,
we presuppose a future in which we will know what goodness and justice are. His work, subtitled "reflections
from a damaged life," suggests that despair itself can be a way of sketching a redeemed world.

flap your wings once, twice
before alighting, let us wake
up sweet and drowsy—perhaps
let us blink, stir ourselves til all
sleep's lovely uncertainties have
faded away and there is only now
you alighting like a warning like
a promise, only faint cries and the
threat of the archer below.

set us on your wings so carefully, we'll
cling to every precious feather and
feel the wind in our faces. the air around
us sounds with shrieks of loss and triumph,
but we are safe here—heads brushing the clouds,
the sky a haven from all figures still & poised
below; we've forgotten what it's like to have someone
sprawled between us and the hunter, what it is like
to feel this precious. oh god it has been so long,
since we were this high.

Sifrei Devarim 314:1
AS AN EAGLE WAKES ITS NEST —
They guided them with mercy and pity like
the eagle which is full of pity towards her
young and does not enter its nest suddenly
— before it beats and flaps with its wings
above its young passing between tree and
tree, between branch and branch, in order
that its young may awake and have enough
strength to receive it.

Rashi on Deuteronomy 32:11
[AS AN EAGLE ...] SPREADETH ABROAD ITS WINGS, TAKETH IT — When it comes to
remove them (the young) from one place to another, it does not take them with its claws, as other birds
do: because other birds are afraid of the eagle that soars so high and flies above them, therefore they
carry them (the young) by their (the mother's) claws for fear of the eagle. But the eagle is afraid only of
an arrow, therefore it carries them (the young) on its wings, saying, "It is better that the arrow pierce
me than that it should pierce my young". So, too, the Holy One, blessed be They, says, (Exodus 19:4)
"I bare you as on eagles wings" (Mekhilta d'Rabbi Yishmael 19:4:3): when the Egyptians marched after
them and overtook them at the Red Sea, they threw arrows and stone missiles at them, whereupon at
once "The angel of God moved ... and came between the camp of Egypt [and the camp of Israel]" that
it might receive the arrows etc. (Exodus 14:19—20).

Your summer ended that day
alone on the mountain
and I wanted to write you a poem
or a song
but I found one already written.
If your words were the rain —
drumming on dead pavement,
feeding flowers in the hills —
let mine be the dew.

It is so hard to remember.
My mother will not tell me,
my elders do not speak,
we are lost with no gods
and this is not your land.

A time of turns
the sky is grey with promise.
No lambs play in the mountains now
and my memory may fail, but today —
today I found your song.

> **Deuteronomy 32:2**
> יַעֲרֹף כַּמָּטָר לִקְחִי
> תִּזַּל כַּטַּל אִמְרָתִי
> כִּשְׂעִירִם עֲלֵי־דֶשֶׁא
> וְכִרְבִיבִים עֲלֵי־עֵשֶׂב:
> May my teaching drip like rain.
> May my speech drop like dew
> like raindrops on grass
> and like showers on the green.

Ve'zot HaBerakha

blessing fell like water
from the hands of our prophet
our river-borne child
as we stood by the river
anxious to cross.

He saw the sea today,
finally. Last promise of a teary
sky, still filled with memories
of the waiting deep.
The rain came today.

Midrash Tannaim on Devarim 34:2

עד הים האח' אל תהי קורא עד הים האח' אלא עד היום האחרון מלמד
שהראה לו המקום משעה שברא את עולמו עד שיחיו המתים:

"Up to the last sea" [Devarim 34:2]: Do not read "up to the last sea,"
but rather, "up to the last day." This teaches that God showed him the
place from the time of the creation of the world,
until when the dead will live.

---

after forty years of shouting myself hoarse I'll use my last breaths to bless you. oh Israel, I wrestled the angel to win your berakha. you can't see my face but I can see yours, all upturned and regretful. know that I can give you all this; know this is all I can give you. I see your whole future and am frightened for you. I see your whole future and I love every ugly bit of you. I look God in the eyes and see all you can be in Their cool, measured stare. I wish you goodbye with a kiss.

Deuteronomy 33:1

וְזֹאת הַבְּרָכָה אֲשֶׁר בֵּרַךְ מֹשֶׁה אִישׁ הָאֱלֹהִים אֶת־בְּנֵי יִשְׂרָאֵל לִפְנֵי מוֹתוֹ:

And this is the blessing with which Moses, man of God, bade the Israelites farewell before he died.

Chizkuni on Deuteronomy 33:1

"And this was the blessing, etc." The letter ו at the beginning of the word וזאת, indicates that the paragraph following is a continuation of what we have read immediately before. Whereas up to now Moses had admonished the people, he now switched to blessing them.

Daat Zekenim on Deuteronomy 33:1

"Before his death": Our sages explain that at the time when the angel of death came in order to take away his soul, Moses took him prisoner (temporarily) and proceeded to bless the tribes each one in order before releasing him.

Sifrei Devarim 357:4

[And God showed Moshe] ALL THE LAND– We are hereby taught that They showed him Eretz Yisrael, settled in its tranquility, and then, belabored by its oppressors.

Rashi on Deuteronomy 34:5

SO MOSHE DIED THERE BY THE COMMAND (lit, MOUTH) OF THE LORD — by the Divine kiss (Moed Katan 28a).

Deuteronomy 34:10

וְלֹא־קָם נָבִיא עוֹד בְּיִשְׂרָאֵל כְּמֹשֶׁה אֲשֶׁר יְדָעוֹ יְהֹוָה פָּנִים אֶל־פָּנִים:

Never again did there arise in Israel a prophet like Moses—whom Hashem knew, face to face.

Printed in the USA
CPSIA information can be obtained
at www.ICGtesting.com
LVHW022016281023
762294LV00005B/34